RO

NAWOK!

'Spread out before us was the wide, green basin of the West Baliem.' (See page 44.)   (*P. Temple*)

Nawok!

THE NEW ZEALAND EXPEDITION TO NEW GUINEA'S HIGHEST MOUNTAINS

by

PHILIP TEMPLE

WITH A COLOURED
FRONTISPIECE,
BLACK-AND-WHITE
PHOTOGRAPHS
AND MAPS

LONDON
J. M. DENT & SONS LTD

To

Puttoh and Duncan

Tim and Dave

and

Lynn

Foreword

by
Sir Edmund Hillary

EXPEDITIONS to the Himalayas and the Andes have become so frequent nowadays that they barely excite comment except amongst the mountaineering fraternity. It is becoming increasingly difficult to find a hilly corner of our globe which has not been thoroughly tramped over by the boots of the climber or explorer. But such corners do exist and this is the story of an adventure into one of them.

The great peaks of New Guinea, with their perpetually snow-clad heads wreathed in cloud near the equator, have interested mountaineers for many years but few have had the energy or courage to tackle the dripping jungles at their feet. This adventurous party has shown us in forthright fashion that these mountains are now accessible, and although final success eluded them on 16,500-foot Carstensz Pyramide their efforts have pioneered the way for other expeditions to come to grips with this tough and challenging mountain range.

Contents

Illustrations

PHOTOGRAPHS

MAPS

Acknowledgments

IN THE midst of all the turmoil and worry of planning and preparation were the people who helped, sympathized and gave advice; the ones who eased the burden, greased the cogs a little.

Our thanks must go to all these people and to those organizations that helped our finances either with cash grants, donation or loan of equipment. To the New Zealand Alpine Club; the Mount Everest Foundation; the Pukeiti Rhododendron Trust; Commercial Bank of Australia Ltd; T.E.A.L.; Royal Netherlands Embassy, Canberra; Royal Netherlands Information Service, Sydney; Royal Netherlands Legation, Wellington; Department for the Central Highlands, Hollandia; Christian and Missionary Alliance; Australian Baptist Field Mission; Mission Aviation Fellowship; Australian Customs Dept, Sydney; I.C.I. of Australia and New Zealand Ltd, Sydney; Sanitarium Health Food Co., Sydney; Skellerup Industries Ltd, Christchurch; Kaiapoi Woollen Mfg Co. Ltd, Christchurch; Mountain Equipment Ltd, Christchurch; Agfa N.Z. Ltd, Christchurch; also Mrs M. Osborn, Mrs C. L. Oaten, Sir Edmund Hillary, Dr. W. F. Otway, Dr J. A. Rattenbury, Dr L. R. Stewart, Captain L. van Rijswijk, J. de Vries, G. Barfoot, R. W. Cawley, R. D. Dick, N. D. Hardie, G. R. Hunter, R. Jones, J. H. Leonard, D. Morgan, F. G. Shaw, L. Warburton and to all others who helped in some way. Finally thanks to Doug Macdonald, who couldn't go, but who saw and nursed the beginning.

Verse extracts are taken from *Arawata Bill* by kind permission of the author, Denis Glover, and the publishers, Pegasus Press of Christchurch, New Zealand.

Prologue

JAN CARSTENSZ could not foresee all the expeditions he would start by discovering the snow mountains of New Guinea in 1623. By 1961 his report had become the prime cause of four of those products of our mountaineering madness. It was inevitable that sooner or later even the peaks of a backwater like New Guinea should receive their attention.

It may have been the snow that beckoned the first expeditions; mere rock was surely insufficient to warrant men pitting their energies against the relentless evils of New Guinea's southern jungles. To tread that snow became the ambition of the inveterate explorer Dr F. R. Wollaston, one of the first Europeans to see Everest from close quarters. He took part in the first and led the second expedition to the unknown Carstensz ranges of Dutch New Guinea.

Guided by the brief entry in Carstensz's log, his British expedition set out in 1911 to reach the peaks from the south coast. After more than a year of struggle they admitted defeat. Jungle and tropical disease took its toll. They were permitted only one brief glimpse of the mountains from a hill twenty miles away. A hard and expensive lesson, it did not stall Wollaston's determination. He returned in 1913 with experience under his belt and launched a more penetrating attack. The hardships of such an expedition can be well imagined. With dying carriers and food shortages he finally reached the foot of the great south wall and, before his desperate position forced him back, he trod the tongue of ice that now bears his name.

With the advent of the First World War the Carstensz shrank into their misty seclusion. Unconquered, their virgin state was forgotten until three Dutchmen mulled over Wollaston's accounts in 1935. Sponsored by the Royal Netherlands Geographical Society, Dr A. H. Colijn laid plans for a third expedition with J. J. Dozy, his geologist, and Flying Officer F. J. Wissel of the

Dutch Navy. Wissel was a key member of this force, tiny compared to Wollaston's carrier armies. They had the modern wonder of the aeroplane and it was this that provided the key to their ultimate success. They arrived on the south coast at the close of 1936 and before setting out waited for Wissel to complete reconnaissance flights to establish the best access route. This he did, discovering a valley to the west of Wollaston's farthest point that broke into the heart of the range and overcame the south wall's formidable defences. Later, after the other two had started up the rivers, he airdropped supplies on the subsequent site of their base camp, dropped them food in the jungle and then caught them up after a forced march.

Colijn went on to lead this small expedition to complete success—almost. They tramped the glaciers and trod the high snow peak of Ngga Poloe, which they thought to be the summit of the range. But the peaks had never been surveyed, and on returning home they found from their calculations that one mountain, which had defeated three attempts, was higher than Ngga Poloe. This was the Carstensz Pyramide, 16,500 feet, which dominates the tremendous south wall with its long, rocky ridges.

Twenty-five years later our expedition began—the fourth, with the unclimbed Pyramide as our objective.

I

Overture

Wicked country, but there might be
Gold in it for all that.

O UR endeavour began, as many other expeditions must, by a
mountain hut. One evening in March, as I lay outside Malte Brun
Hut and watched the setting sun splash crimson over Mount
Cook, I pondered the words of that indefatigable mountain
explorer, Eric Shipton: 'Things have a way of panning out so long
as one knows what one wants.'

I wanted to go to New Guinea, but so many things seemed to
be in the way—lack of money, lack of experience and, above all,
lack of knowledge. Just what and where were those snow peaks
I had heard about?

My companion that day did not think much of the idea and
gave me a second-hand description of rain and mountains covered
in scrub. But I doubted his pessimism. The doubt sparked an
optimism which was such an important part of all our planning,
optimism in our insolvency and when we faltered in finding the
way.

When I returned to Christchurch after a glorious week of
climbing by the Tasman Glacier, I celebrated my twenty-first
birthday by writing away for more clues. I discovered Wollaston's
account of the first expedition to the Carstensz and was searching
for routes from the south coast when I encountered David
Cooper of Auckland, who had also discovered the peaks and
wanted to go in 1961. So we combined, and over the following

months combed New Zealand for information and painfully pieced together the puzzle of the Carstensz.

David, an industrial chemist aged thirty-two, had spent most of his spare time in the previous dozen years tramping and climbing. His tall, fair-haired, thickset figure was well known in the Waitakeres of the North Island and at Milford Sound in the South. Dave brought the qualities of an industrial chemist to his planning in his meticulous thoroughness. His special province was food and by the time we left we were all looking forward to our diet of 3,670 calories, 460 grammes of carbohydrate and 18 milligrammes of iron per day. Responsible for our health, he went even further and assiduously practised his hypodermic needle technique. He graduated from basic training on oranges until—the sight will always be recalled in North Auckland of a stuck pig squealing across a yard, hypodermic waving from its rump.

From Dave's research came the important information that access to the Carstensz was possible from the north. He discovered that a mission station existed about five days' travel to the north of the range and, best of all, that it had an airstrip. This seemed much better than the three or four weeks' trip from the south coast that Colijn had made, and it offered the prospect of un-explored country. The northern high country, which we came to know as 'the plateau', remained a mystery to the day we set foot on it, and its effectiveness as a route was always in doubt. Later we heard lurid tales from people who had flown over the area: tales of 'vertical walls' or 'horrible, broken country', and even to the day we left Hollandia the southern route was recommended to us. But mountaineers are independent people and the prospect of discovery lured us on.

Such information came slowly, and it was only after we established contact with people in Dutch New Guinea that we could lay a firm foundation for our time-table and planning. It was at this early stage that our party of six came together. Dave invited Tim Barfoot, also thirty-two, his close friend and com-panion of the hills. Tim, short and powerful, was an amateur weight-lifter and canoeist as well as mountaineer, and he enlivened many an evening's tent talk with tales of record lifts and meets on the Wanganui River. An estate agent, he found our jungle trek gave him few opportunities to study the intricacies of native freeholdings and mortgage.

The third member, Duncan Dow, accepted Dave's invitation and immediately strengthened our prospects of success. Duncan, aged thirty, was a geologist at Wau, Australian New Guinea. He was a veteran of many trips into the New Guinea highlands and his knowledge of conditions and native peoples was to prove invaluable. Tall, dark and sparsely built, he proved the greatest goer of us all. Although we cursed him at the time, we can thank him now for his relentless 'Nawok!' ('Get moving!') which kept us going through the listless days of mud and rain.

It was about this time that the need was felt for a leader to cox the Christchurch and Auckland oars of the expedition boat. Not content to be spread over New Zealand and New Guinea we looked farther afield to Australia. Through the good offices of Norman Hardie, on his way to the Himalaya at the end of 1960, we found our man. Colin Putt, aged thirty-three, lived in Sydney, where he had been inexplicably exiled for some years. His interest in mountains had never been lost, despite the flattened vista of the Australian countryside, and he accepted our offer of leadership with alacrity. Throughout his long service as chairman and later secretary of the Australian section of the New Zealand Alpine Club, he had always harboured hopes of a trip to New Guinea. Puttoh, as he was known among the climbing fraternity, was big, over six feet tall with a fourteen-stone frame to match. His pack-carrying feats were notorious and his lift of a 120-pound load over unexplored ridges in the Blue Mountains will be long remembered in Sydney bushwalking circles. Puttoh's special forte was invention. An engineer, his mind hummed with new ideas for constructing tents, strengthening ice-axes or dehydrating meat. He made his own parka, pack and trousers. He spent weeks in the construction of our transceiver radio, yet carried with aplomb all the worries of an expedition leader. Puttoh had climbed not only in New Zealand and tramped in Australia but had spent seasons in the Welsh hills and Swiss Alps. He numbers among his exploits a traverse of four peaks in one day, while his New Zealand habit of cutting many large steps on an ice climb led him to be taken as a guide by a local professional. As might be expected, he was also a sailor, and the stories from his youth spent on Auckland mullet boats were always a guarantee of laughter.

The second Christchurch member was Lynn Crawford, fresh from success in the Andes. With Lindsay Stewart and Dal Ryan of Invercargill he had reached the summit of Nevado Cayesh, a difficult 18,770-foot peak in Peru, which had defeated Swiss and American expeditions. Although still worried by a frostbitten toe, he had little hesitation in accepting my invitation a scant three months before we left at the beginning of June 1961. Aged twenty-three, Lynn was a carpenter-climber, building huts and an enviable reputation as climber in the shadow of Mount Cook. Of medium height, dark and well built, he exhibited an unfailing good humour under the worst of conditions.

Finally, myself, a New Zealander of only four years' standing who emigrated from London to discover climbing and the glories of the Southern Alps. Aged twenty-two, I worked fitfully at publishing and public relations before finding my feet in mountains and writing.

For non-New Zealanders it will give a better appreciation of our disposition if I ask them to imagine the leader in London with two members in Hamburg, a further two in Helsinki and a sixth on the scene of the crime in, say, the Caucasus. Needless to say, the expedition's main hazard was writer's cramp. We had a heavy mail and I wondered when starting this account whether or not publication of our letters would suffice instead of a book. There were enough, and their story would be almost as interesting.

Jobs were handed out equally. Puttoh got his teeth into paperwork, radio, survey and red tape; Duncan looked after geological and carrier preparations; Tim and Dave dived into food, pills and botany. That left me with equipment and, somehow, finance. Looking back, I realize that I volunteered to be treasurer and can only put it down to a misguided enthusiasm.

The expedition came perilously close to financial disaster before it began. Our spirit of optimism almost failed when our twenty-three cases of freight sailed for Australia with a third of our budget unfound. An eleventh-hour cable brought news of our main grant and my finger-nails were allowed to grow again. We hoped to keep our expenditure low and were surprisingly successful—I was never any good at figures.

The bare frame of the expedition slowly filled in as information accumulated. Dave had been able to find Colijn's book on the 1936 trip and its wealth of photographs began to give us a clear picture of the range.

The mountains are arranged in a horseshoe, lying east to west, with a large glacier in the middle. Sheer walls from 4,000 feet to 10,000 feet high deny access on all sides save the west: there the glacier had broken through hundreds of years ago, bending towards the south, and in retreating giving a perfect pass into the heart of the shoe. It was this break that Wissel discovered on his aerial reconnaissance. It was accessible only from the south, however, and we faced the task of broaching the 4,000-foot Noordwand, whose approaches were unknown.

Within five days' travel of the Noordwand lay the American mission and airstrip of Ilaga. This was the key to the approach from the north. Without the use of that airstrip, or a similar one in the vicinity, a direct approach from the north would have been impossible, involving at least a three weeks' march from either the Wissel Lakes or Wamena in the Baliem Valley. We based our planning on the use of Ilaga and for flying us in we contacted the Mission Aviation Fellowship.

The M.A.F., as we came to know it, is a dedicated band of American fliers closely associated with New Guinea Protestant missions—in particular with the Christian and Missionary Alliance. Flying from dawn to dusk six days a week, its small, single-engined aircraft provide a lifeline to the isolated highland mission stations. Supply by normal methods along mountain tracks would take days, weeks or even months, using an immense amount of time and labour. The steep grass airstrips and the little monoplanes save the missionaries' time and energy for more important work.

We contacted David Steiger, manager of the M.A.F., and he agreed to fly us in. This brought up the question of airdrops— were we going to carry a ton of food and equipment with us or use the well-tried Southern Alps technique of airdrops? The use of light aircraft in the mountains was commonplace to us, while Dave and I had in the past used ski-planes to good effect. We found that M.A.F. skipdropped supplies from fifteen feet as a matter of course. Doubting the value of native carriers, we had few qualms in pencilling in a time-table of drops.

Airdrops meant taking radio to give the pilots weather and position checks. The appalling cost and weight of efficient transceivers threw us back on our own resources and Puttoh was soon hard at work designing and constructing a lightweight transistorized set. With the help of an electronics engineer he spent weeks of spare time fiddling with transistors, soldering wires and redesigning circuits until he produced an impressive, hand-generated machine weighing only seventeen pounds. In its first test in Sydney it jammed Radio Australia: giving us false confidence in its New Guinea ability.

We were helped at every stage of our preparations by the New Zealand Alpine Club. Apart from a generous donation to our funds we were given free access to the club's expedition equipment pool. This solved many problems. We took as much personal equipment as possible, but that did not solve the expense of tents, down jackets and ropes. The club lent us all these plus many smaller items and saved us the expenditure of £500. We had become royally equipped, and included in our baggage were Meade tents that had been to the Himalayas and Andes and down jackets from the Antarctic. Doubts were expressed on the need of down jackets four degrees off the equator, but they proved a blessing in disguise.

Information seeped in like the drip of a Chinese torture. After reading translations of the relevant sections of Colijn's book we were still in the dark about the northern plateau. We read short reports of missionaries who had travelled across the plateau and crossed the main divide not far east of the Carstensz, but not one threw any light on the terrain—in fact it was possible that they did not cross the plateau at all but travelled in river valleys farther north.

Through correspondence with the chief pilot of Dutch New Guinea's commercial airline, De Kroonduif, we heard that a prospecting expedition had followed Colijn's route to the Carstensz in 1959 searching for copper and gold. A letter from its leader yielded the vague news that the northern approaches 'looked most uninviting' with 'a vertical north wall'.

Maps of course were few and far between. The sketch maps we did obtain were hopelessly inaccurate. A series of aerial survey maps produced by the U.S. Air Force during the war proved useful at the finish but were unavailable for larger sections of our trek. We gave up in disgust but our despair was tempered by the prospect of extensive exploration.

The beginning of 1961 saw the intensification of Indonesian claims to West New Guinea, or 'West Irian', as they renamed it. A small guerrilla force was landed on the south coast to create a nuisance but was soon rounded up by the local tribesmen. The outlook of having to contend with Indonesian guerrillas and possibly hostile, and obviously capable, natives, gave us serious food for thought. We decided to include two shotguns, a revolver and a variety of ammunition for shooting duck and other game.

The pressure of preparations came to a head at the beginning of April. Despite terrifying mishaps, our twenty-three assorted cases left Auckland and Christchurch on 11th April and duly reached Sydney in good time. From there they were shipped for Hollandia on 17th May.

I left for Sydney, as the advance guard, on 26th April, clutching a handful of tin openers that I had forgotten to buy. As the Teal jetprop vibrated across the moonlit Tasman Sea I consciously relaxed for the first time in weeks, smoking a chain of cigarettes during the four hours' flight, for I had too suddenly nothing to do.

Passing through the customs at Mascot Airport I already felt the loss of two hours' sleep, but on meeting Puttoh again after more than a year all sleepiness vanished at the thought that this was the first sign of the expedition's coming together as a unit. I threw my gear into the back of his jalopy and we roared through town—Puttoh clearing traffic with a clamour of bugling. We talked ceaselessly of radio, airdrops, freight and visas: visas in particular. They had come through in New Zealand with little delay but there was an Australian fly in the ointment. A bond of £500 was necessary before we would be allowed into New Guinea. Through Puttoh's efforts this was found, but not before a great straining of our resources.

With the bond to the Netherlands Embassy went each member's 'Personal Information' sheets giving the lowdown on his disabilities. The sheets presented a list of awkwardly translated questions culminating in a droll 'Are you getting into contact with the police?'

The three weeks in Sydney were a period of frustration. False starts with radio construction and failure to raise the expedition to a state of profit by a television contract were only offset by seeing the freight on its way to New Guinea. During their period of transhipment the cases were stored in Puttoh's garage to save money and were secured by customs seals. I had to restrain my eagerness to show him our equipment prizes until Hollandia.

Our frustration was further increased by the receipt of a letter from Mr Steiger informing us that we would not be able to land at Ilaga. It appeared that the airstrip belonged to the Christian and Missionary Alliance with which M.A.F. was closely affiliated. They had sole ownership of the strip (the Netherlands New Guinea Government had no jurisdiction over missions) and were averse to our use of it. The reasons were not clear. The expedition picture darkened, especially when he mentioned that an alternative route from the Baliem valley was populated by natives 'whose fad is to kill any strangers'. I went for a get-fit tramp in the Blue Mountains, leaving Puttoh to the vagaries of radio and the worries of Ilaga.

The last lap of the preparations began when I flew from Sydney on 22nd May bound for the final problems in Hollandia. We flew everywhere, finding it cheaper in the long run and infinitely faster. Time was the all-important factor as both Puttoh and Dave were limited to a six weeks' time-table starting 4th June. I therefore aimed to make arrangements that cut delay to the minimum.

The giant jet DC-8 climbed to the north. The endless arid wastes of the Australian interior unrolled before us like a carpet. At 36,000 feet we cruised over the Arafura Sea until, five hours from take-off, the curved, low-lying coastline of New Guinea swam imperceptibly out of the haze. Knowing our route passed only slightly west of the Carstensz I rushed to the starboard windows as the first line of trees whistled past far below. But after a few minutes I returned to my seat rubbing my eyes, aching from the glare of sunlight reflected off the masses of billowing cloud which covered the highlands. The Carstensz clutched tight its mystery.

Soon Biak appeared out of the rain at Geelvink Bay. Our huge, awkward bird angled for landing.

2

Manyana

I've tea and sugar and flour,
And inside the hour
I'm heading into the hills.

IT WAS winter and the dry season, but no sooner had I stepped out of the air-conditioned cabin into puddles of recent rain than heat swept into my face and coiled slowly up my legs. I sweated and cursed silently in jacket and heavy raincoat as I passed through the haphazard customs, and trudged with my typewriter and bags to 't'Rif', the K.L.M. hotel and Biak's façade to international air travellers. The DC-8 bellowed in the background and then screamed off the long runway into the throat of a brilliant sunset. It made a grand finale to the first stage of my journey. I wasted no time in placing myself strategically beneath a huge, slow-moving fan with a cool drink. I relaxed and watched through the lounge doors as the fishermen in their catamarans slid home across the evening calm on the bay; their backdrop of sullen blue-black rain clouds merged into the rising hills of the main island and then disappeared into the night.

Since Ilaga was unavailable it was my duty to explore every possible route into the Carstensz from the north. A likely alternative was from the Wissel Lakes. This would entail flying from Biak, and that night I met officials of De Kroonduif. Seated in an air-conditioned office, like a refrigerator after the sultry evening outside, I listened to details of flying times, costs, payloads and schedules that did not add up to anything more than a last-resort plan. Costs were too high and schedules too variable to make the

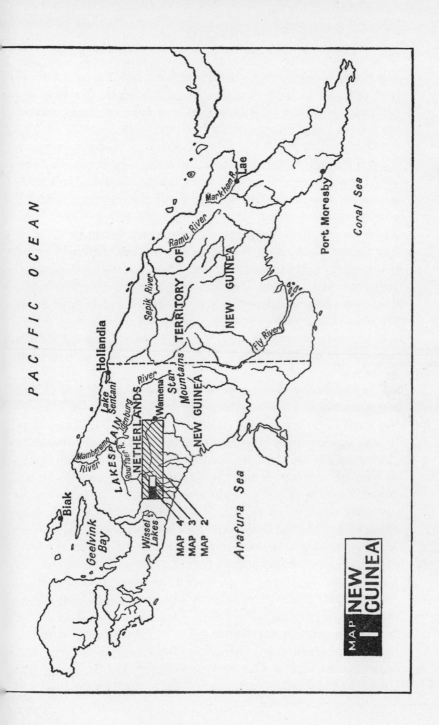

MAP
NEW
GUINEA

1

Wissel Lakes route worthy of serious consideration. The idea
was finally scrapped when I learned later that it would take at
least three weeks from the lakes to the Carstensz. The first day
had been inconclusive, with neither a view of the range nor an
advance in flying arrangements.

't'Rif', which had been shipped out from Holland in pieces
for lack of native craftsmanship, provided a good night's sleep
until I was disturbed at 4.30 a.m. to catch the plane for Hollandia.
There was a soothing lack of urgency in the preparation of the
aircraft against a silent, flickering background of naked flares
which kept the lowering mists off the runway. When we climbed
into the half-dark cloud forty-five minutes late, we had learned
that this was a country of no time. There was no sophistication
about the twin-engined Dakota. Bare stringers were the cabin
lining, on which condensation rapidly formed and dripped on to
my arms. The windows soon misted up but it made little difference, the view consisting only of swampy coastline and a sudden
panorama of the Mamberamo River sweeping on a flooded front
to the sea.

After landing at Sentani airfield the first problem was to find
accommodation. I was told that the hotel in Hollandia, twenty-
five miles away, was fully booked by a Dutch parliamentary fact-
finding mission, and I was feeling desperate as the airport rapidly
cleared and the few taxis disappeared down the road. Jacob (Jaab)
de Vries came to my rescue. The inland fisheries officer for Dutch
New Guinea, he saw my plight and generously offered room in
his house close by the airfield. This was the start for him of an
episode on which he must look back with mixed feelings. In an
act of generosity he unwittingly took many of the labours of the
expedition on his back, and we must be eternally grateful to him
for his help. Beginning with myself he accepted twenty-three
cases and two drums of freight on his front veranda and, a fortnight later, five more unholy New Zealanders.

As if to give me forewarning of the trip to come, it rained
heavily and steadily as I carried my bags into Jaab's house and
took my first look at Dutch tropical living. His bungalow was
similar to many others in Sentani, lying lower than the road and

from any distance away almost invisible behind the long grass. Brick-built, the wide eaves of its roof encompassed lounge, kitchen, office and two mosquito-proofed bedrooms. I was soon made at home with my first can of Dutch beer. Jaab, tall, broad, fair but bronzed, spoke excellent English like most of his compatriots. I felt ashamed as typical of the English-speaking man who had never raised the energy to learn a second language. Malay is the lingua franca in coastal Dutch New Guinea, and his expertness at this as well as Dutch and English made his help as interpreter invaluable.

Although miles from Hollandia my position by the airfield put me within close proximity of David Steiger and the Christian and Missionary Alliance (C.A.M.A.). When I heard of this I wasted little time and saw Steiger that first morning. Slight and fair, his modest demeanour belied his flying experience and ability as he listened patiently to the hare-brained alternatives to Ilaga that I laid before him. I suggested a floatplane landing on a lake close to the range or, to save time on the return, that we clear an airstrip for him to take us out. His gentle explanations soon relegated those ideas to where they belonged. I was left with the simple situation that a landing at a mission airstrip, somewhere, was imperative. He explained that one of the reasons why C.A.M.A. did not wish to see us land at Ilaga was the annual C.A.M.A. conference, which would take the resident missionary away at the time we would be passing through. An added difficulty arose in that Steiger would be heavily employed at the same time, carrying missionaries from all over the island to their conference centre in the Baliem Valley. This was the first sign that our transport arrangements were in jeopardy.

That night I was taken to the local cinema which, like most public buildings and shops in Sentani, was housed in a Quonset hut left over from U.S. occupation during the war. There are constant reminders of the great Base 'G' which served as General MacArthur's headquarters and supply centre before the reconquest of the Philippines. Rusting landing craft still litter the harbours, old jeeps and G.M.C. trucks still clatter along the American-built roads, and the foundations of MacArthur's headquarters are still visible above Ifaar, the former Seventh Fleet Recreation Center, which is now occupied by Dutch marines. We drove along an abandoned, pot-holed taxiway close by the air-field, crossed a fighter dispersal apron and went into the Quonset to endure a fourth-rate American film with Dutch sub-titles.

Early the following morning I went to Mission Hill, where the headquarters of C.A.M.A. were situated. There I laid our case before the field chairman and manager, the Rev. Harold Catto. It soon became apparent that the chief stumbling-block at Ilaga was not the conference but the bitter taste of an earlier ornithological expedition, which had abused the privileges of landing at the mission. The C.A.M.A. committee were wary of our application. I furnished a letter guaranteeing the expedition's morals and swift passage through Ilaga and asked for reconsideration of our application. This was agreed to, but required the circulation of the letter to committee members who were spread far and wide in the interior. Due to flying delays and indifference the letter did not leave within the following fortnight and last-minute altera-tions to plans had to be made when the rest of the party arrived. Of this I was happily oblivious at the time and left for a trip to Hollandia in high hopes of a speedy solution to the problem.

Between Sentani and Hollandia are the Cyclops Mountains, pushing their steep, jungle-clad ridges to over 7,000 feet and creating an effective barrier to direct travel. Begun by the Japanese, a sealed road was completed by the Americans linking the airfield at Sentani to the Hollandia harbours, and it was along this that I travelled for the first time that afternoon. Over the following two weeks I drove up and down it to the extent of a thousand miles and came to know every jungle-fringed bend and all the hills with sudden views. It followed the edge of Lake Sentani for some distance, winding round the little bays with their lakeside restaurants and villages. Passing over the eastern spurs of the Cyclops, the road climbed to the magnificent view of Jautefa and Humboldt Bays before dropping steeply to the town, clustered on the harbour hillsides. Jaab took the course at breakneck speed in his rattling jeep, scaring brightly dressed Papuans on to the grass verges. The coastal Papuans, a lazy, smiling people, never seemed to realize that a road was basically for motor vehicles. Many times I rounded corners during the following days to find them strung across the road with their loads of bananas or sweet potatoes, or even taking a catnap on the edge.

After forty minutes we threaded through the town traffic and it was not long before I paid my first official call at the Government offices. I received unfailing courtesy to the extent of being loaned a Land Rover for the period of my stay. That solved the transport problem to Sentani. Buses and taxis were respectively too unreliable and too expensive; to be independently motorized was a godsend.

Before the offices and shops shut down at 2 p.m. I was able to jump my first fence in customs procedures and have my first look at this town, which had been completely destroyed during the war and rebuilt from scratch. It was a curious mixture. The sparkle of new Government offices was offset by the hulk of a landing craft in the water a few yards away, and the shining New Guinea Council building stood not far from the untidy litter of Chinese trading stores. It seemed that the chance to rebuild Hollandia on a methodically planned basis had been wasted after its destruction; it was already a hotchpotch of slow Dutch development and rapid Chinese or Malay exploitation. A conglomeration of weeds and flowers had grown up among the burnt-out stumps of the past and cried aloud for some gardening.

The two-o'clock rush hour was a revelation. The people lived under the basic tenet of *manyana* (tomorrow will do), but their working hours from 7 a.m. stultified its practice and the release at 2 p.m. sent the scores of air-cooled cars and vans scurrying off like bees to honey. Only one lane of the roads was filled with these vehicles: the lane leading to bungalows, bays and siesta. I was in constant opposition to the local value of time. With dozens of details and arrangements to attend to within the short period before the main party arrived, I seethed silently at 'Tomorrow is soon enough' or 'There is still plenty of time'. Trying to mount an expedition in such an atmosphere, I felt like a shark among the bathers.

But for the moment I indulged in a little *manyana* myself.

Jaab took me away from the two-o'clock bustle to a beach hidden at the Pacific limit of the coastal road. There was a bar secreted among the palms and I sipped contentedly at a cool drink, watching the surf break on a reef while Jaab told me his fish problems and plans. Later, after a meal, we drove back home into the dusk. By Lake Sentani an illuminated beer sign gleamed illogically from the verge of the jungle, and then we were surprised asa gang of children jumped out from the bushes and whooped as we roared past. Back at Sentani I wrote up my diary against the shrill evening chatter of cicadas, and in writing, suddenly realized that after three days in New Guinea I was little further ahead than I had been weeks previously in Sydney. 'One has to adopt the philosophical attitude,' Duncan would reiterate later, but I could not help feeling that preparing the expedition was like winding up a clockwork engine, slowly, patiently, yet knowing that it would run down just as fast.

As May drew to a close plans developed slowly but surely. I fell into the rhythm of Hollandia life, and although I still bucked vigorously against delays I succumbed to the relentless tropical time-table. Each day was marked by an early rise to savour the morning freshness and a shower to wash away the fetid night. After a light breakfast, the stimulating drive to town through a cool breeze would put me in a bright frame of mind to meet the rigours of expedition business. During the morning as I paid my calls the heat would build up; my recollections of Hollandia during the day are of scorching sunlight with dark havens of restaurants and bars. I was told that it was the cool, dry season, and as I watched the heat shimmer along the roads I shuddered at the thought of the hot, wet months.

Early on I obtained our gun permits, opened an account at the one bank and arranged radio schedules with the telegraph department. The *Sibigo* docked on time on 26th May and I saw a little miracle as our cases and drums, garishly painted in expedition colours of red, green and black, swung safely on to the wharf, all intact and none missing. The cases containing supplies for air-dropping were painted red, and these, the majority, were stored in a shed ready for special packing by the shipping company. The

(Photo: P. Temple)
Colin Putt

(Photo: P. Temple)
Duncan Dow

(Photo: P. Temple)
David Cooper

(Photo: T. Barfoot)
Tim Barfoot

(Photo: P. Temple)
Lynn Crawford

(Photo: L. S. Crawford)
Philip Temple

Wamena, the site of the only Government post in the Baliem. *See* page 24.
(*P. Temple*)

Many of the Danis were minus one or more fingers. *See* page 30. (*D. E. Cooper*)

rest I had delivered to Sentani, where I began the hopeless task of sorting.

Initially I tried to work in the early afternoon on returning from Hollandia, but as the sweat poured off my brow and I gasped for breath after prizing one case nail loose, I reconciled myself to lazy afternoons with cool drinks and light reading. Slowly I accepted the siesta and soon happily dozed my afternoons away until, in the cool of the evening, I could attack the cases with renewed energy.

The problem of packing was a major one: not until the last few days before leaving could I reach decisions on where we would be starting from and with how many native carriers, if any. Knowledge of carriers in Hollandia was surprisingly vague. Even those who had travelled in the highlands supplied conflicting information. I learned that the people in our area were of the Dani tribe, but just how many would be likely to come with us, how much and what food they would require, and how much they should be paid, was impossible to discover. I did find out that their load-carrying capacity was limited to thirty-five pounds, and accordingly divided supplies for the march into twenty-two piles of that weight. Later I was assured that Danis would eat rice and fish and that huge quantities of their normal food, sweet potato, would be unnecessary. Armed with this assurance I bought 660 pounds of rice and 640 tins of fish. The bulk of this was delivered to the store where airdrop packing was under way. After I had carefully weighed out quantities for each airdrop load it was carefully sewn into double rice sacks.

The days disappeared with no decision on Ilaga. C.A.M.A. displayed little interest in our plans. My frequent calls at Mission Hill met with indifference stiffened by a disguised resolution to bar access to Ilaga. This attitude was inexplicable. I could do nothing to overcome it, though our case was made clear and all manner of guarantees assured. I began to cast round desperately for an alternative. Tiom appeared in the planning, a mission station in the Baliem valley. Although ninety miles farther away from the Carstensz than Ilaga, it was an Australian Baptist mission and would feel none of the influence of C.A.M.A. I was

c

also deluded into thinking from my sketchy maps that a direct route was possible from Tiom, by-passing Ilaga in a long traverse of the plateau. I applied for permission to land at Tiom as a safeguard against the Ilaga negotiations falling through.

An attack of jaundice limited my view to the worsening aspects of the expedition. I found that no clear petrol was available in Hollandia for our spirit stoves; an M.A.F. plane broke down, throwing their schedules in chaos and jeopardizing our flying and dropping arrangements once more. Reports of native wars came from the interior. When the doctor suggested I spend a few weeks in bed with my illness, I almost went home.

The expedition simmered in the hot sun and warm rain. The Carstensz became unreal and lost in the maze of frustrations. I could visualize Puttoh, Dave, Tim and Lynn counting the hours to the finish of their work and packing eagerly in the cool sanity of Australia and New Zealand, in preparation for a sticky, chaotic start to their trip. What a miserable place Hollandia became, what a godforsaken country!

One evening broke into my anxiety with release. I went to a children's film show in Hollandia—a film of the expedition to the Star Mountains in 1959. My Land Rover hissed along the now familiar road streaming with rain, windscreen wipers performing valiantly against a powerful evening shower. On reaching the crest of the road by Jautefa Bay, where the rain ceased, I stopped to gaze at the fresh, star-covered view. The moon had crept round the fast-fleeing cumulus cloud and now illumined the graceful, lagoon-like bay, which passed through a narrow entrance into the Pacific reaches of Humboldt Bay. From the arm of land dividing the two bays, lines of glimmering fishermen's huts graced the water like luminous pearls.

The film show was held at the police barracks in an open-sided hall with the inevitable bar and chocolate counter at the rear. Hundreds of Papuan, Malay and Chinese children chattered under the jurisdiction of a teenage overseer, who brandished a big stick and shouted to little effect when the screen flickered into life. It was difficult to understand why it was a children's show; the films were largely of the New Guinea Council elections and all were in Dutch. But one film was a general survey of Hollandia, and excited screams and yells filled the air as the children's friends, parents and teachers appeared. Westerns seem to be the most popular films among the Papuans, and a few teenagers slouched around the hall parading jeans, loud shirts, and cowpunchers' hats in an attempt to make the films more acceptable by their presence. The expedition film came last. I watched enviously as helicopters and a variety of aircraft pushed the sixteen-man team through the jungle. Six of them finally reached the snowy crest of Juliana Top. I left refreshed and reassured that climbing a snow mountain in New Guinea was not impossible after all.

With the beginning of June the jaundice passed and the time for decision came. Ilaga was no nearer our grasp than it had ever been and I began to plan exclusively on an approach from Tiom. Suddenly I was informed that carriers would be almost impossible to obtain for a journey to the high country and that they certainly would *not* eat rice and fish. I chewed my fingers in indecision as I viewed the beautifully prepared airdrop sacks and the Papuan boys carefully putting the last stitches in after days of steady work. I could hardly muster the courage to tell the overseer that most of the sacks would have to be unpicked, emptied and all the carrier food returned to the suppliers, but it had to be done. The food was returned and I advanced to the Chinese Toko or general store to discuss the reimbursement of my hundred pounds' worth of cheques. I emerged a grease spot after seemingly hours of harangue and argument, all in Malay and completely unintelligible. Apart from my terse exchanges with the man who supplied my order the rest consisted of screams between him, the proprietor, and the proprietor's wife, who insisted on bawling in my ear in an effort to intimidate me out of my cheques. I kept a firm grip on the counter piled with repulsive, evil-looking food until the grubby cheques found my pocket, then I fled leaving the bedlam behind.

Duncan arrived on Sunday, 4th June. This eased the situation considerably and proved once more that two heads are better than one. Armed with his freshness to the problem we approached C.A.M.A. again in the hope of retrieving the Ilaga plan. It was to no avail. We formulated a new plan, which involved carrying our own loads from Tiom. Try as we may, we could not cut down the six loads to anything less than sixty pounds, and the plan included an airdrop of food five days out and the main drop ten days out. We felt tired at the thought of it but nothing else could be done.

The pace quickened with the other four members of the party due on Tuesday, and Monday saw our attempts to synchronize our plans with airline time-tables. The flight bringing the boys in from Biak was due at 9.30 a.m., the flight to Wamena in the Baliem valley was scheduled to leave at 10 a.m., and M.A.F. would ferry us from Wamena to Tiom starting at 11 a.m. But in order to obtain final permission to land at Tiom, Puttoh had to see the secretary of the mission, who was due in from the interior at 10 a.m. Delaying tactics were required somewhere and we placed our implicit faith in De Kroonduif to run late. They did us handsomely—they never flew to Wamena at all. *Manyana.*

The delay in flying to Wamena gave us the opportunity to settle down as a six-man expedition at last and leisure in which to untangle the final worries. With everyone together the planning became more realistic and six heads proved better than two. The fuel problem had been solved by Puttoh bringing two kerosene stoves. We filled up our polythene jars with seven gallons of kerosene and one gallon of ordinary petrol to be airdropped for the one spirit burner we needed for high camps. We obtained final permission to land at Tiom and the stage was set.

With the thought of carrying our own loads through largely unknown country we pruned equipment drastically. From the original decision to carry three two-man tents and one four-man tent we dropped to one four-man tent and a sheet of plastic fly; for cooking we were to rely largely on wood fires and included only one kerosene stove with one gallon of fuel—our utensils were one pressure cooker and two billies. Anything that was remotely superfluous was tossed out of the pile on Jaab's lawn. We limited ourselves to one shotgun and revolver with a minimum of ammunition, one nylon rope, a communal towel and soap, three headlamps with one battery refill and six candles. Our only luxury was down jackets which we decided to take instead of sweaters; otherwise clothing was limited to one complete outfit with a spare shirt and socks. With our clothes, share of equipment and five days' food pushed into our trusty Mountain Mules, we weighed our loads and grimaced in silence as the spring balance jerked regularly to sixty pounds and over.

After final discussions, flying arrangements were crystallized. On Friday, 9th June, we would fly to Wamena, leaving our airdrop supplies there before M.A.F. flew us to Tiom. From Tiom we would attempt to reach the Carstensz by as direct a route as possible, receiving a food airdrop five days after leaving if carriers were unobtainable and the main drop as directed by radio.

On Friday we watched our loads being carried into the aircraft and could hardly believe that the expedition was about to be born. The flight was virtually an expedition monopoly. The double seats of the Dakota were bolted to the starboard floor, making room for our pile of sacks lining the port side of the cabin. As we swung aboard with our clanking ice-axes the few other passengers carefully seated themselves at the far end of the plane. We took off, climbed and banked to the south, and suddenly all the frustrations of the past weeks were forgotten.

3

The Pass of Arrows

Rivers swell and twist
Like a torturer's fist.

THE ripples of the coastal hills were left behind and we droned over the wide expanse of the Lakesplain. This huge basin, an extension of the Sepik-Ramu-Markham Depression of Australian New Guinea, harbours the great sweeps of the Idenburg and Rouffaer rivers. These join to form the Mamberamo and present a river system to rival that of the Fly in Papua. As we flew, the Idenburg curled and swept below, appearing and disappearing between the little piles of white cumulus and presenting a fantastic picture of ox-bow lake, river terrace and meander. Occasionally a tiny village clearing broke the endless vista of olive-green jungle and swinging water. This plain, or swamp, as Lakesplain implies, forms a barrier to the Baliem valley that only air transport can penetrate.

After half an hour the range hiding the Baliem valley loomed ahead. The Star Mountains were strung out to the east with Juliana Top's little dome of snow incongruous above the mass of green forest and contorted limestone. Instead of gaining height to clear the range we broke through a gap past immense white precipices, scraped the forest and suddenly swept over the broad, cleared plain of the Grand Baliem valley. To the south, Wilhelmina Top, 15,800 feet, stood like a guardian over the sweet-potato fields. After one circle the aircraft dropped and bounced along the grass airstrip of Wamena, the site of the only Government post in the Baliem. It lay a few miles from the river itself at

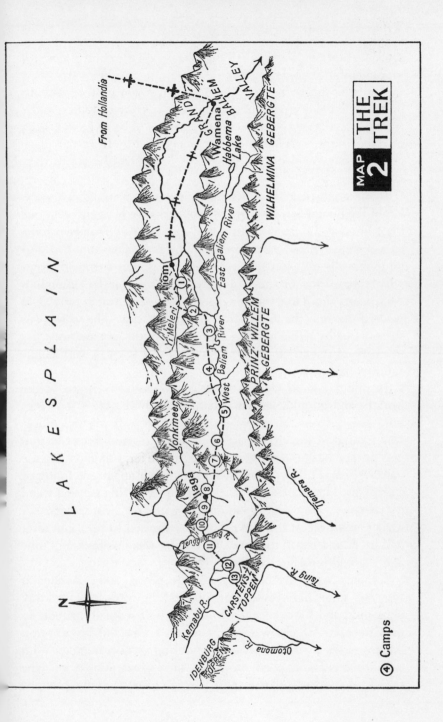

N

LAKES PLAIN

From Hollandia

GRAND VALLEY

Namena
Habbema BALIEM
Lake VALLEY

WILHELMINA GEBERGTE

East Baliem River

Yimeleni

Vonkmeer

Baliem River

West Baliem River

PRINZ WILLEM GEBERGTE

Naga

Tenggilorong R.

Ijeamera R.

Kemabu R.

Tsing R.

IDENBURG TOPPEN

CARSTENSZ TOPPEN

Otomona R.

MAP
2
THE
TREK

④ Camps

5,500 feet on the Wamena tributary and was the control post for a population of 50,000 natives.

The atmosphere was hardly an improvement on the insidious heat and humidity of Sentani, and attempts at collecting one's thoughts and energy at first were fruitless. The sacks had been unceremoniously dumped barely twenty yards from the plane and were surrounded by a throng of little Dani boys and their fathers.

If the atmosphere was little different the surroundings were. From the bungalows and cars of Hollandia we had moved in one brief hour to the thatched huts and *kepewaks* of Wamena. Even so we were cheated of complete transition. The huts had aluminium walls and a jeep laboured over the grassless row of humps which passed for a road. The huts, with the shining aluminium edifice of the Government hostel, spread haphazardly and petered out into the dusty, treeless countryside. The valley was surrounded by hills and cliffs, narrowing to the east and west. As the Dakota roared off for home we felt our last link with civilization tangibly cut.

In one corner of the airstrip a single-engined Cessna of the M.A.F. and its pilot waited patiently until we sorted ourselves out. This proved easier than expected. Once the district officer was located in the crowd, we were able to hand over our gun permits and health certificates and begin the ferry to Tiom, up the valley. First Puttoh, Duncan and Lynn disappeared, followed shortly by Tim and Dave in a second plane, leaving me sticky and fly-pestered, wondering what to do with our airdrop sacks. A Malay employee of the Government promised to help, but after half an hour I began to worry. A Cessna was due back any time and it could not afford to wait.

I soon tired of grinning Danis, who peered and marvelled at my two huge black eyes (sun glasses) or took lights off my cigarettes, and I was relieved to see a jeep eventually trundle in my direction. A trailer was handy but the connecting pin was not. This was discovered after more shouting than searching. With whoops the Danis piled the sacks in a great jumble into the trailer. We drove off the strip and crawled painfully past the hostel to a shed. Everything was stacked out of the weather. As I pushed the last sack into place I thought fondly of tinned fruit on cool mountain tops; no premonition of the disappointment to come jarred my anticipation.

The 9th of June seemed to be our day. As the Cessna swung to a stop on the steep strip at Tiom I was greeted by a circle of Danis and the news that we had carriers for the journey to— Ilaga! A weight was taken off our minds as well as off our backs. 'Just need to carry your camera,' David Steiger grinned before he took off.

The carriers would agree only to a journey to Ilaga, with the result that a direct plateau route to the Carstensz was impossible. The Danis wished to keep to well-beaten tracks with a definite objective in view: mountains meant nothing to them. Moreover, no supplies of sweet potato would be available on a direct route, and this fact finally ruled out such a plan. A trek to Ilaga made C.A.M.A. objections pointless. Our hand was forced with no alternative in view and we had to gamble on the unavoidable transit through Ilaga meeting with C.A.M.A. approval.

Fourteen carriers had been obtained, eight to travel through to Ilaga and six to see us on our way for two days. Food tins were being opened and bargains struck. The eight Danis for Ilaga agreed to carry for one large bush-knife each. These knives were left in the custody of the Baptist Mission to be given to the men on receipt of a note from us showing that they had fulfilled their contract. For the two-day carriers, beads and cowrie shells would suffice as payment.

Exchanging *koanas*, I surveyed our eight new companions for the trek. All were of similar height, about 5 feet 8 inches, but there, save for their common race and language, the similarity ended. Their facial features were as diverse as any European race, ranging from Semitic through Polynesian to Assyrian. Typical of their tribe, they were solidly independent both as a group and as individuals. The white man was not their master but their tutor; the atmosphere was not one of servility but one of tolerance and co-operation.

The individualism of the Dani tribe was marked by their

variety of 'dress'. The common factor was the *kepewak*, a gourd penis-sheath, but there was no standard and they came in a variety of shapes, lengths and widths. Yellow, they were supported from the hips by a single strand of bark fibre (or string) and occasionally sported a decoration on the tip.

Hair was arranged in many ways, with head-nets (*petari*) common, supplemented by feathers and any coloured materials they could obtain. Two outstanding examples of head decoration were encountered later at Ilaga. One Dani wore a highly coloured tea-cosy while another, with the most elaborate hair-do we had encountered, sported the packet top of a patent hair perm. (Which twin?)

Beads were strung round every neck, while arm- or waist-bands were often favoured. Painted faces seemed to be a matter of taste. Elaborate colouring was found only among the hierarchy, and on special occasions, but blackened foreheads or cheeks were common.

Nose bones and beards were rare and it was fitting that the leader of our carriers, Ijomba, should have both. White and curved downwards, his bone lent him an air of ferocity, strengthened by the large steel axe he slung over his shoulder. This could not have been more misleading. A God-fearing Christian of the first order, he displayed great intelligence, wisdom and honesty and set us an example by holding prayer-sessions regularly three times a day. He marshalled his troops well and there was little dissension either among themselves or with us throughout the whole trip. In fact, their good humour and easy-going natures often smoothed our path of thorns. Ijomba, aged about forty, was older than the rest, who ranged from a boy of fourteen to men of thirty.

We made the carriers' loads up to thirty-five pounds in yellow kit-bags or sacks, leaving thirty pounds each for ourselves. Before we left we looked over the mission and marvelled at its extent, all buildings erected by the missionaries themselves with hammer, saw and nail and inexperienced native labour. A hospital was in course of construction, and a sawmill, already in operation, showed the first mark of industry in the area.

We parted regretfully with the mission's hospitality and early afternoon tea, and, clutching lists of Dani words, hoped that we should make ourselves intelligible.

The trek started at 2.30 p.m. as Ijomba hared off up the hill behind the mission carrying a Mountain Mule. The temperature and the pace were hot. After half an hour's tramp we realized that our original intention to carry sixty pounds had been preposterous. The switchback tracks, humid climate and our unfitness would have finished us off on the first day. Besides, we did not know the way. It came as something of a surprise to find that we did not back-track to the Baliem, which as yet we had only seen from the air, but headed up a side valley, the Yi-Meleri. Nevertheless we were going in the right direction, due west.

We had little idea of what lay ahead and fondly imagined that two days would see us on a broad, rocky plateau. Here we would 'travel like greased lightning', to quote one who had observed from the air. On such information we had based an estimate of five days to Ilaga. But as yet we gave little thought to something two days ahead; our eyes and minds were preoccupied with a new and absorbing country.

Led by Ijomba, the Danis bobbed along the meandering track balancing kit-bags and sacks on their heads and shoulders. The track was rough, largely of clay, and went up and over the spurs leading down to the true left bank of the river. It never contoured to the hills, rising 2,000 feet above our heads, but fell constantly to streams and rivulets. The lower slopes were potato fields with clumps of casuarina trees and long grass, whilst higher up forest still prevailed with occasional timber clearings. At intervals we would pass through a village of three or four huts well fenced to keep enemies out and the pigs in.

The party gradually spread out over a quarter of a mile and regular stops were necessary to let the bobbing yellow kit-bags or heaving green mules catch up. Dave was still suffering from the after-effects of a leg broken the previous October and the going did nothing to help his stiffness.

With the lengthening shadows the day became cooler. It felt

good to be in old, loose clothing once more, listening to the noise of a fast river and a tree breeze. The general scene was similar to New Zealand bush country but the signs of strange and primitive habitation spoke of no ordinary New Zealand trip but of the culmination of fourteen months' planning and anticipation.

Women were working in the fields, scraping with sticks for potatoes. They would pause and stare as we passed and *koanas* would float through the afternoon air. Our carriers stopped friends along the track to tell them proudly of their *tuans* and the journey on which they were setting out. As we passed, a smile, handshake and *koana* were the order of the day and by evening we had an inkling of royalty's ordeal. Many of the Danis were minus one or more fingers, cut off in repentance or mourning, and it was disconcerting to accept their flabby, incomplete handshake.

A couple of hours after leaving Tiom we stopped in one of the potato fields and purchased *mbi* (sweet potato) for the carriers. Old, wizened women brought *jums* (net bags) of twisted, pink potatoes and tipped them on the track for scrutiny. After some confusion and bargaining enough was accumulated, and Duncan, who was rapidly coming into his own as native expert, doled out payments of beads. The women held out large, thick leaves in the palms of their hands and stared with faint smiles of satisfaction as spoonfuls of tiny coloured beads were emptied on to them. Then, clutching their treasure, they happily slung the empty *jums* over their foreheads and returned to their digging.

As evening came we approached a gorge. The villages were left behind, the bush thickened and the roar of the river over its boulders grew louder, echoing heavily up the hillside. Still on the true left bank we came to a vine bridge slung across the water. We gingerly crossed the swaying strands, our packs awkward and ice-axes getting entangled in the stays. We did not travel much farther but descended to a grassy flat in the mouth of the gorge, where we camped.

It had been a good day. As I struggled for the first time with our four-man Meade tent it seemed impossible that we could have achieved such a complete transition within one day: from comparative civilization to a slightly known valley in the highlands of New Guinea. I felt very satisfied as the smoke from three fires curled into the windless evening. A crescent moon was lodged in the trees, there had been no rain, it was a perfect camp site.

We celebrated this successful first day by diving into the river for a bathe. Whether this would rate with any of H. W. Tilman's 'memorable bathes' or not is hard to say. It was certainly memorable for us because it was our first and last before Ilaga. Tim lost our only cake of soap. The Danis were intrigued by our antics and gathered along the bank as the collection of white bodies pranced up and down in the cold water.

The Danis lit two fires that night, and since no rain threatened did not bother to erect a shelter: when it grew cold they just crawled head first into the sacks. They threw *mbi* on to roast and settled down to a chattering which continued into the early hours of the morning. No doubt they discussed the *tuans* and the strange and wonderful implements they carried with them. Duncan spent some time after dinner talking with them and demonstrating the use of our equipment. They thought the tent a great idea but in particular were fascinated by our headlamps. A torch was entirely new to them and shouts of delight shattered the night as beams of light flicked on and off among the trees.

As I wrote my diary that night I had an appreciative audience in a Dani whom I christened 'The Irishman' for his gift of the gab. He sat beside me for some time watching as I produced blue squiggles on the sheets of strange white leaves. As we ate our dinner of stew he regaled us with stories of enemies further up the valley who would chop off their heads. The other carriers listened in dead silence. That was the cue for our demonstration, and with Dave emulating a howling savage I shot him dead with a mute revolver and Puttoh brandished the shotgun.

With their fears apparently allayed they returned to their fires and unceasing babble. Later they sang a little and as I fell asleep the sound of their dirge-like chanting filled the tent.

'Nawok! Nawok!' Ijomba's deep-throated shout echoed through the dew-filled gorge as we started up the steep track towards the sunlight. He stood on the narrow path, axe on shoulder, and watched as the last of the carriers reluctantly picked up their loads, hunching their shoulders against the morning chill.

The camp had lost its charm of the night before and we left the damp ashes and trampled grass to the unseeing river. We gained height quickly to warm our limbs and break in our wind. We met the sun at an outcrop of rocks and bathed in its warmth as it crept slowly down into the gloom. We rested there, waiting for the stragglers to catch up, and saw the head of the valley. Ijomba put down his mule and gestured vigorously at the hills to the south-west. Forcefully he described our route to come, removing his nose bone to make conversation easier. The Irishman added his piece, but it was only after Duncan's halting questions from the limited list of words in his hand that any information was understood. The valley widened after the gorge before narrowing once more in its swing to the north-west. To the south-west high, forest-covered hills limited our view, and it was over these we had to climb higher up the valley. We would cross a pass into the Baliem.

When the party was together once more we sidled down into the valley and began the daily exchange of *koanas*. Behind us a boy stood silhouetted on the hillside and watched silently as we descended through the first potato fields and scrambled over stiles or slid along muddy paths. We crossed the river again on a tree-hidden vine bridge and followed the water's edge before climbing to more fields. To shake hands and say hallo was a good excuse for a rest and I took advantage of it as the sun became hotter and the sweat of unfitness trickled down my chest and back. I met a party of Danis, who carefully stood to one side as I stumbled past in my heavy boots. My greeting was cut short by the squalls of a baby, apparently from the bushes behind them. Curiously I peered around their bare backs and was amazed to to hear the plaintive cries issuing from the bottom of a boy's *jum* filled with food. The boy smiled. 'Koana!'

Before we reached a village the children would come to meet us, dancing down the paths from nowhere with shouts and laughter. But as they came near us they would stop silent and unsure until we glanced at them; then their faces would wreath in smiles as we cried 'koana'. Tumbling under our feet, they would lead us over the stiles to the huts and then cluster in thoughtful speculation before remembering their joy. Like pied pipers we would draw them with us away from home until a new crowd from a new village would meet us and fill the gap as the last children melted away. We grew fond of their sparkling eyes and happy faces and were sorry to lose them later in the day when the villages were left behind.

After an hour's travel that morning we reached a village of four huts set high on a spur overlooking the river. From here we had a comprehensive view back down the valley and could see how the cultivation had diminished as we travelled. Several hundred feet lower in the distance we identified the hill of the Tiom mission, the cleared hillsides widening to meet it. Beyond, the high walls of the Grand Baliem were visible and the twisted, unusual peaks of the Star Mountains. Our pass to the Baliem was now much closer and Ijomba decided that at this village supplies of the staple sweet potato should be bought for the remainder of the journey. We gathered that this was the last friendly village, although the significance of that information did not impress itself upon us until later in the day.

We dropped our loads and waited for the villagers to bring out their food for Ijomba's inspection. It was typical of the Dani villages we had passed through—circular huts with walls of strong bark and wood, about three feet high and topped by a thatched grass roof. Each hut boasted only one opening through which people, light, air and smoke had to pass. I peered into one, and as my eyes became accustomed to the gloom, pitch black after the bright sunlight, I saw a group of women working round a small fire, its smoke hanging heavily in the roof. Young women had been rare during our walk and when I noticed two or three hidden in the hut I began to understand why. There was obviously a distinct lack of faith in the morals of six strange *tuans*.

Needless to say, the hut was quite bare. There was no furniture, no bunks or raised sleeping shelves. Blankets or cloth of any kind were non-existent since there is no native plant from which fibres can be drawn. The hut was simply a shelter from the rain and darkness with only meagre comfort emanating from the smoky fire.

The Danis' lack of craftsmanship was becoming rapidly apparent. We did not come across any drawing or carving, no matter how crude, and they had not progressed even to the manufacture of cooking or water vessels. A few gourds were their only type of container, hence our discarded tin cans were seized almost before they left our hands. There was no scene here, familiar in African travelogues, of women gracefully balancing pitchers of water on their heads.

They did, however, make their *jums*, which were similar to the English housewife's string bag. They were not made from string but from bark fibres which had been painstakingly woven together and then shaped into a net. Although generally brown in colour, some had bands of yellowed netting. The *jum* was carrier-bag, potato sack and suitcase all rolled into one and loads of up to forty pounds were supported in them by two simple loops over the forehead. Rarely, armbands were made from plaited fibres.

The village compound was trampled mud in which varying sizes of domesticated black pig snuffled, occasionally harried by a single dingo-like and barkless dog. The village and its group of fields were surrounded by stout fences up to five feet high constructed of logs and sticks securely bound with bark fibres. They proved amazingly strong, amazingly numerous, and we spent much of our time clambering over stiles. The vile stinks and smells that I had anticipated near villages had materialized only in small doses and the acrid smell of carrier sweat soon passed unnoticed in our own muddy vapours. A bare skin had its advantages in that kind of country.

The villagers squatted behind little piles of sweet potato and maize waiting for inspection of their goods. Their headman sat aloof and to one side with a token offering of one or two potatoes before him. He watched with a suitably bored expression as the negotiations went on and did not bat an eyelid as *tuans* clustered round to photograph his feathers and paint. Danis still came running along the tracks from near and far bearing loads of potatoes in the hope of procuring some precious beads. In close consultation with Ijomba, Duncan paid for a growing mound of

The women held out large, thick leaves in the palms of their hands to receive coloured beads in exchange for sweet potatoes. *See* page 30. (*D. E. Cooper*)

A village set in a prominent position on a spur overlooking the Yi Meleri River between Camps 1 and 2. *See* page 33. (*P. Temple*)

A village above the Yi Meleri River between Camps 1 and 2. Circular huts with walls of strong bark and wood about 3 ft high and topped by a thatched grass roof. *See* page 33. (*P. Temple*)

Varying sizes of domesticated black pig snuffled. At a village above the Yi Meleri River. *See* page 34. (*P. Temple*)

food. We were not rich in beads or shells and a few small bags had to last the trip. Beads were used as payment for food and small services while one cowrie shell would buy one man's labour for a day. These small, white shells were extremely valuable in the highlands; the older and more worn they were, the higher their value.

The carriers stuffed their *jums* with food and, turning away late traders, we made preparations to leave. Before we moved Ijomba held prayers and the sixty or so natives squatted with heads bowed and eyes tightly shut as he stood and spoke. We joined in and listened to the uneven flow of his words. Occasionally he would falter, to be prompted by a voice in the congregation, but would continue with the same speed and earnestness until his speech was rounded by a common 'Amen'. We looked at this amazing man afresh. Completely untouched by vanity or power he spread a benevolent and forceful influence over all the Danis we encountered, and proved in all his actions and prayers that he was a Christian of probably more faith than and as much understanding as ourselves. He never ordered his men but led the party with a quiet wisdom and infinite knowledge of the country and its vicissitudes.

Before we could continue the trek we had to sort our carriers out from the little crowd of hangers-on who sought to infiltrate into our party for a few days to claim the reward of shells. Although we would have gladly taken on more carriers our economy and the problem of food supply would not stand it. We had reluctantly to sort the wheat from the chaff. Duncan called out the almost unpronounceable names of the Tiom carriers and lined them up with their loads, but even after that one Dani persisted in his efforts to go with us to Ilaga. He pleaded with Ijomba, clutching his few worldly possessions and pushing his little pig and pregnant wife to the fore. We let him come since his opportunities to migrate to Ilaga were few and far between. It was safe to travel across the hostile country ahead only in large parties, and these were rare: we were a guarantee of his safety. 'The Pigman', as he came to be known, proved an asset to the party and one of its best carriers.

D

We continued on up the narrowing valley along the switch-back tracks and ditches, splashing through tributaries and looking forward to the next stop out of the sun. Two hours later we crossed the Meleri yet again and stopped by a shady stream for lunch. The Danis lit fires and we soon had tea-billies boiling to minister to our parched bodies. Dave brought out his water-filter and after half an hour of careful manipulation produced cool, chlorinated water for our lemon crystals. We were still in a highly disorganized state and it was many days before it was unnecessary to untie all the kit-bags and sacks in search of tea or biscuits. We usually made do with what we could find.

Our final crossing of the Yi-Meleri took place early that afternoon, when we waded to the knees and approached the foot of our hill and pass. As I looked up to the towering mass of forest I shuddered at the thought of the stiff climb to come, and it was perhaps this thought that made me lag behind the vanguard of the party. As I tramped through the first belt of trees a shot rang out, a dull boom muffled in the thick, oppressive air and lowering clouds.

I quickened my step and as I emerged from the trees I was greeted by our fleeing carriers, loads scattered over the hillside below the village and excited shouts filling the air. Gesticulating, they pointed to a more courageous group surrounding Puttoh and Duncan by the fence. Perplexed, I dropped my pack, pulled out Duncan's revolver and, after stuffing bullets into the chamber, raced up the hill. I passed Lynn busily retrieving arrows from the bushes and then stared past a cursing Puttoh at a group of warriors prancing on a hill, bows and arrows in their waving hands. Duncan, a little pale, grabbed the revolver and obviously felt better with the feel of it in his hand. In the fore he had missed a clutch of arrows fired at him, dodging them as they floated through the air. Ijomba, typically unperturbed, assessed the situation, while Puttoh continued to curse in his efforts to eject the spent cartridge from the shotgun.

Ijomba unwittingly had led us into an ambush. The attackers, whose land we intended to pass through, had seen us coming from afar; in the hope of an easy robbery they had waylaid us. Our weapons were packed away and not readily accessible, but Puttoh's smart assembly of the gun and quick shot over their heads had soon put them to flight.

They now shouted and threatened from a safe distance. This was fortunate since we were temporarily defenceless. The shot-gun ejector had jammed and Duncan's revolver was full of the wrong size of bullet. We decided not to stretch our luck and under Ijomba's direction we made a detour round the village. The carriers had regained their confidence but stuck close to the ineffectual shotgun as we started the climb to the moss forest. We climbed steadily through the last furrows in the fields and were soon swallowed up in the safe embrace of dripping and oozing branches.

We had been prepared for the gloom of the moss forest by thick grey clouds which had threatened and darkened the country-side since early afternoon. Before us stretched the wall of tangled green swathed and cushioned by spongy moss. Vines strangled the massive trunks, searching for light in the roof of leaves. Roots fought for living room and nourishment in the steep mud. There was an aura of petrified struggle as the vegetation lay locked in soft yet deadly embrace, a grim hostility that estranged the birds and pervaded the air with unnatural silence. Streams trickled quietly over beds of dead leaves or muffled their roar in tunnels of decay. The silence affected our own movements as we climbed, softening our footfalls in the mud.

We all climbed differently: Duncan smoothly from years of New Guinea travel, Puttoh heavily with an air of determination and still clutching the shotgun, Lynn quietly and steadily. Behind my efforts to achieve a flow in my movements, Tim came in unrhythmical rushes while Dave climbed carefully, nursing his leg. Our laboured breath floated in momentary clouds of vapour in the chill, saturated atmosphere. The carriers with their pre-hensile toes balanced gracefully up the jumble and stairway of roots and left us behind, but continued to guide us with a steady stream of hoots and calls that gradually faded above.

Unfitness and height began to tell. We had little time for rests, for the proposed site of Camp Two was over the pass, which seemed to get no nearer as each rare gap in the foliage showed more hill and more forest. When we did rest I snatched gratefully at a cigarette, Duncan scribbled in his geological notebook and Puttoh sat restless and always silently annoyed at the need to stop. Half a cigarette—and we were away again in the relentless upward plod.

The track, no more than a cleft through the forest, was littered with fallen trees notched by the Danis to aid the grip of their toes. I was at a distinct disadvantage in heavy rubber-soled boots and my efforts to retain balance along the lengthy traverses of slimy, inclined wood ended in careens into the undergrowth. My pack was welcomed at last as it cushioned the falls.

The carriers came back without their loads; taking our packs, they encouraged us on to a clear outcrop of rock, where we sat in fading sunlight. The rock was almost pure quartzite which had Duncan baffled as he hammered away for a specimen. We had gained considerable height from the deep 'V' of the valley below. This was the reward for our labours and we estimated that we had reached 9,000 feet. With only three hours of daylight left we could not pause for long. We had a short respite of open, rocky ground before plunging once more into the trees. I dropped steadily behind Puttoh, Duncan and Lynn, who tramped in close file, at times almost machine-like as they drew ahead.

The pass came unexpectedly through the trees, at the top of an open patch of soggy tussock. I pulled myself in stages to the crest, pausing regularly to bend over my ice-axe and regain my breath. I took in the new view, looking eagerly for signs of the plateau or the wide reaches of the Baliem River. But there was nothing save an endless crumple of dark green hills and flat, grey cloud. There was no sign of life, no clearings, no villages, just a vista of dank forest. Dully I squelched down into the twilight, following the bare footprints and bootmarks in the mud. As I made voluntary and involuntary glissades down the track, the carriers with Dave hooted from above me, steadily, until there was an answer from below rising faintly like a bird call through the evening. Overhead thunder rumbled in the sullen sky.

I burst through the trees into open swamp and high grass. The lower shouts grew louder and shortly two figures came hurrying towards me, one proudly with a lamp on his head. One of the Danis stopped to shoulder my pack while the other rushed on to find Dave. Still full of energy the carrier led me on; soon we breasted a rise and saw a column of blue smoke rising from the damp hollow of our second camp.

Beside the limp, sagging tent the carriers had a large, sturdy *kanangda* (hut), where they crowded round a roaring fire and roasted their supper. How they managed to talk and eat in the thick pall of smoke is hard to understand, but they presented a happier and warmer picture than our own efforts at supper as we groped among damp kit-bags in the dark. My stomach wanted little of food that night and after soup and a few mouthfuls of stew I tipped the remainder discreetly away. I crawled into the end of the tent and fell into a solid, dreamless sleep as soon as my head touched the floor.

Our position that night was unknown. We knew simply that we had left the Meleri and had crossed a range to the south-west in the general direction of the Baliem valley. How far the Baliem was, if the plateau existed, and where the Carstensz lay, were matters of complete guesswork. We had to trust Ijomba implicitly to lead us on a safe and direct route to Ilaga. Hostile territory was not yet behind us, and on the following days 'Tuan Boom' as Puttoh was known after the attack, had to lead with the shotgun ready. The ejector had been repaired and Duncan's revolver was properly loaded.

Any apprehension we may have harboured about the honesty and reliability of the Dani carriers was banished by Camp Two. They carried well, lit our fires, brought water and were concerned about our welfare. The Australian Baptists had done a good job in their conversion.

The 11th of June was a Sunday but it made little difference to our wet and misty surroundings. We had a big breakfast to make up for any lack the night before and started the day with a stiff climb. This brought warmth and exercise to our tired muscles. A steep start to the day always seemed to be best, breaking in our wind early and making the rest of the day better by comparison.

The moss dripped more than ever as a low mist wafted through the trees and a rough hand on a branch often shook a drenching shower down one's neck.

We emerged from the climb into open, tarn-covered tops before dropping on the south-west side of the spur towards a wide valley that opened out in the distance. Through an occasional opening in the trees a high range showed its bare limestone crest rising into the belly of the cloud, but otherwise nothing but trees and more trees. No bird song broke the sound of squelching bare feet and boots, or the muttered curse as someone slipped on a slimy root and went up to his calf in mud.

The Pigman was having a hard time. His little black hog found the mud and roots just a bit too good to be true and his exhortations were of no avail as the poor creature struggled vainly with logs twice its height. When the pig slowed up too much he casually shoved it into the bottom of his rice sack and the forest silence was broken with squeals and loud grunts as the animal gasped for air. But the weight of the pig became too much for the Pigman with his other load. Lynn, in a rash moment of pity, took the pig from him and strapped it under the flap of his Mountain Mule. The maker of the pack can claim yet another use for his product.

We stopped for morning tea in a wide, flat clearing and learned that here the short-term carriers would have to leave us. This caused a stern reappraisal of the loads. From now onwards we should all have to carry our packs, where before one or two *tuans* had been relieved of theirs. Not only that, we were reduced to eight men and our loads would certainly be increased. We laid the food out on the grass and transferred as much as possible from tins to plastic bags. A small amount of fuel was discarded. Little else could be thrown away and we groaned in dismay as we slung on our packs, now topping forty pounds in weight. Duncan gave the departing carriers their beads and shells and without wasting time they shouted *koanas* and disappeared into the trees.

A steeper descent followed before we began to contour along the sides of the wide, forested valley. The day became more and more monotonous, my pack heavier and my boots, thickly caked in old and new mud, like lumps of lead. As a glimmer of sunlight shot through the leaves far above, it suddenly occurred to me that we had experienced no rain. Looking at the dripping vegetation, I guessed we would not be spared for long.

The monotony was broken as the Irishman, walking in front of me, suddenly stopped and with a vigorous display axed away the foliage to our left. 'Balim!' he proudly announced, pointing, and sure enough, hundreds of feet below, the great Baliem River curled slowly to the east through the forest. This sight put more power in my stride. An hour later we sidled down and out on to the swampy verges of the river.

4

The River of Mud

But the mountains on the rim of the day
Have nothing to say.

Beyond the broken-down *kanangda* the river with its lazy brown reaches formed a barrier to any further progress to the south-west. It was the first real signpost of the trek, innocuous looking yet deep and powerful, forcing our track due west towards its source.

The *kanangda* suggested lunch and we lay in the open on the drier grass warmed by the sun and the thought that the first, decisive stage of the journey had been completed. We were committed. Any doubts, any physical cringing, any fears as to the efficiency of our plans were beyond recognition.

From our position deep in a valley of endless trees the idea of the plateau with its promised 'broadness and rockiness' was something of a joke. The suggestion, too, that we would be able to travel 'like greased lightning' was only true to the extent that it was greased liberally with mud. I had been the chief exponent of the plateau's existence and was mercilessly ragged as our journey showed more trees and plastic tracks.

Steep overgrown banks stopped us from following the river's edge. We descended only to climb once more into the forest. The brief, illuminating interlude by the water was soon swallowed in the panting, heaving business of more 'Nawok!' Increasingly the forest became broken by clearings dotted with deserted huts and overgrown gardens, and we encountered again the switchback tracks over the furrows we thought we had done with in the

Meleri. Ijomba intimated hostile country ahead and told us that these villages had been abandoned as a result of wars: wars of revenge that had cleared the beautiful, peaceful clearings above the river. Ijomba, by now out of view of an appreciative audience, had removed his nose bone for good and only returned to it when we reached Ilaga. He had given his steel axe over to another Dani and his staff of leadership became Duncan's new Italian ice-axe, which he normally carried on his head, firmly clasped with both hands.

In our traverse above the river we passed without seeing the point at which it goes underground—'The Hole in the Wall'. Few white men had seen this phenomenon and we regretted that our tight time-table did not permit a detour. We were compensated, however, by a reproduction in miniature. The tumble of a wide stream, flashing among trees beyond a clearing, brought visions of being able to wash away the mud that encased our legs to the knees. This was not to be: a natural bridge about ten feet wide spanned the water scores of feet below and denied us this luxury but shortened the climb up the next hill.

The vegetation was curiously lacking in flowers. The occasional sight of a small red blossom would trigger Dave to careful photography, manoeuvring with close-up lens and light meter. Dave was the botanist of the expedition but had to forego study *en route* or risk being left behind in the relentless tramp to reach the next camp by nightfall. We could not pick and choose our camp sites. A *kanangda* for the Danis had to be found and invariably one would never appear until well into the afternoon; they seemed to be strategically placed at day intervals like primitive hotels with plenty of firewood and running cold water. The day had grown hotter and the grey blanket of the morning had been replaced by billowy white clouds. As we lay stretched full out for a rest, drinking fruit squash from our water bottles, my mind's eye transformed the scene into a comfortable couch and a cool Dutch beer. It seemed incredible, but that had been our lot only three days previously.

We stumbled down, back towards the river. Breaking from the forest we crossed a deep stream spanned by a rickety collection of logs and sticks and waited under the lee of a grassy hill until the whole party was across. Ijomba indicated that Puttoh should go first with the gun and then we filed quietly up the hillside to its crest.

Spread out before us was the wide, green basin of the West Baliem. The steep, forested range which had dominated our southern view all day petered out into the basin and from behind it came the East Baliem River to make its junction with the great meanders of the western branch. The backbone of the island was fully visible at last. Almost completely embraced by dark scrub, the range pushed clear nevertheless with limestone slabs, blocks and pinnacles. The all-important view to the west was hidden by low spurs transgressing into the heart of the lush green country-side. Towards the far southern side of the basin, beyond clumps of trees, a thin spiral of blue smoke rose untroubled into the late afternoon sky. The silence was oppressive.

Ijomba trod warily along the hillbound track above the swampy river slopes in close company with 'Tuan Boom'. We crossed a few streams before reaching an open knoll with an unrestricted view on all sides save the north. There a *kanangda* was secreted in the trees and Ijomba pronounced Camp Three. The importance of the open view became apparent when the carriers imitated the vigorous chopping of axes and flexed their arms with non-existent bows and arrows. There were now two or three fires across the basin that to me seemed highly suspicious. Dani hut or cooking fires rarely gave off enough smoke to create pillars visible for miles, and their sudden appearance suggested a signal of our arrival. With the tent up, the Irishman, who could have graced any stage with confidence, mimed the arrival of enemies up the hillside who crept beneath the tent eaves and made off silently with the kit-bags. We took him at his word and before going to sleep piled up the loads in front of the tent door.

The Danis soon had a fire going with a facility born of long practice and ingenuity. Before we gave them supplies of matches they used embers carefully wrapped in several layers of thick leaves, and with prodigious blowing powers they soon trans-formed dull red ashes into a blazing pile of logs. We were lazy, and without making any effort on reaching camp at nights would simply yell 'Kani!' and a fire would soon appear to dry our socks and toes. Another yell of 'Yi!' and our billies, rapidly blackening with soot, hissed for a brew of tea.

The speed with which we obtained fire or water depended on who yelled. Tim, Dave, Lynn and I faded into insignificance in the carriers' eyes alongside Puttoh or Duncan. Duncan, with his stock of beads and shells and experienced dealings with them, commanded a high degree of respect, as did Puttoh with his long boom and white *jum* (string vest). Communication with them became progressively easier as they grew to understand our requirements and eccentricities. Our limited list of Dani words contained only two verbs, *nawok* for get going and *nogo*, meaning sleep, which soon became synonymous with camp. Mime and demonstration filled the gaps in our language range. It was impossible, of course, to explain to them our motives in making the journey. We did not learn the word for mountains until much later. Our strange implements, such as ice-axes and packs, coupled with a lack of Christian fervour, must have been perplexing to them. Earlier they fondled our ice-axes and equipment with wonder but rapidly took all for granted. No doubt they had become resigned to the strange purposes of the white man.

The sun went down on another rainless day and darkness hid the wide East Baliem Valley. The smoking fires across the river brought a false sense of security. With not enough room in the *kanangda*, one or two of the Danis stayed by our cooking fire and turned our socks as they dried. All our socks were indelibly stained a rusty red from pigments in the mud and eventually even our feet took on an unnatural pink. No other clothing required drying at this stage, but I indulged in a complete change from drill shirt and trousers to a track suit, releasing my calves from their sticky sheaths and my back from the damp circle of sweat. All the others wore shorts until the colder regions near the Carstensz but I persevered with longs. Although distasteful to draw wet cloth over one's legs early on cold and misty mornings, they did save me from the sores and cuts that the others sustained. To keep the worst of the mud out of our boots we wore strong canvas gaiters made by Puttoh. Originally designed as snakeproof gaiters to counter the common ankle- or calf-bite, they were never put to the test, as snakes were never seen, but they served admirably against the mud.

As a final precaution Puttoh decided to sleep with the shotgun by his side and wear everything save his boots to be ready for any kind of emergency. This met with everyone's approval except Dave's. He had decided to sleep out in his sleeping-bag cover among the pile of kit-bags and was afraid that his regular nocturnal short walks would arouse Puttoh to some dangerous sleep-walking.

Puttoh got up rubbing a hip sore from the pressure of a pocketful of cartridges. There had not been a whisper during the night and hordes of thieving natives had been lost in heavy sleep. The morning was full of cloud, damp and silent, swirling around the ridges to the west as if purposely shrouding the view, holding its unknown quality till the last possible minute.

I did not feel too stiff and tired as I swung on my pack after a good breakfast. I was approaching a state something like fitness; the prospect of a day's tramp no longer filled me with abhorrence modified by resignation, but tinged my outlook with pleasant anticipation. This was ground away later in the day but at that moment the muddy exploration was more than worth while.

The others must have been feeling the same because we set off at a fast pace around 7.30 a.m., continuing along the banks of the river about a couple of hundred feet above the water. We were now in an extensive depopulated area. As the deserted gardens widened the track became increasingly furrowed and old fences with rickety stiles appeared. Between each clearing were belts of moss forest where the track dissolved into mud and pools. At each successive line of trees Ijomba grew increasingly anxious and with Puttoh would scout ahead, gingerly tiptoeing through the long grass to peer carefully into the undergrowth. He would go down the track out of view for a short way and then reappear with the all-clear sign. Obviously we were reaching an important enemy stronghold, but there were no signs of hostile activity no matter how hard we looked among the trees or across the river.

About two hours after leaving camp we came to a stretch of swamp. We balanced along partly submerged branches, plunging in to our knees at any false step: thus we regained the familiar slush of the forest with relief. We halted by a dry spot at the edge of the swamp where the Danis made morning tea. This was their custom at every major stop since they seemed to derive satisfaction and comfort from a small, smoky blaze. They never had much trouble lighting fires. Taking a handful of dry grass from the bottom of their *jums* they would light and manipulate it until there was a blaze in their hands, then it would be transferred to a pile of dry twigs and sticks. They soon had enough flames to put on logs, and when these had burnt down to a glowing redness they roasted sweet potato.

The carriers were marching well, setting the pace, though their loads were somewhat lighter than ours. The Pigman's pregnant wife went as fast as any during the first days even though she carried the full load of family possessions, while her husband took a swag from us. He humped the pig, which Lynn had rapidly discarded after an hour or two the previous day. Lynn had been ensnared, and though he was relieved of the pig he had to carry the Pigman's satchel of belongings and spare *kepewaks* instead. Most of the Danis had little satchels made of wide yellow pandanus leaves bound together and folded to contain their more important possessions such as beads.

The sun began to break through the greyness and threw a more cheerful light on the limited, monotonous view. Where were all the exotic orchids and brilliantly plumed birds we had been told to expect? Now and then a small, blue, swallow-like bird swooped silently among the trees; the forest twilight was pierced by solitary and tiny blue or red flowers; but there was no massive display of colour. We could only put down the lack to the season and decided that the winter must have driven the birds to the warmer coastal areas. The lack of life was disappointing and seemed unnatural; the lack of wind a deathly stillness that claimed everything.

Ijomba held prayers before we started off. We guessed that this held some significance, remembering a similar set of prayers shortly before the attack in the Meleri. When we emerged from the next neck of trees we were confronted by a long, tall palisade, which showed signs of much better maintenance than any previous fence since the Meleri. On climbing to the top we saw that the palisade formed a semicircle with its base on the river. To the left was a hut with smoke seeping through the thatch, and just visible through the bushes an impressive vine bridge that bellied down towards the swirl of the Baliem. A lone native came from the hut to meet us, unarmed and with a reluctant air as thought it were a distasteful duty. *Koanas* were made but his handshake was half-hearted and he looked us up and down, then over our shoulders as more of our carriers arrived. He kept conversation with Ijomba to the minimum. Puttoh leaned carefully on the shotgun while Duncan nonchalantly twirled the chamber of the revolver. This had the desired effect. Our welcomer's look changed to one of appraisal, and so to fear and shiftiness. He soon said goodbye and trotted back to his hut, which was obviously the sentry point for guarding the one means of crossing the Baliem safely. He must have passed on a sobering report to his superiors since from that point on we met no signs of hostility, or even people, until we had almost reached Ilaga.

Nevertheless I clambered over the awkward palisade at the western end of the compound feeling a disconcerting itch in the middle of my back, for I momentarily provided a lumbering, defenceless target for a native arrow. As after the Meleri attack, we welcomed the enclosure of the forest and forgot the mud for a while.

Reaching an open hilltop we were able to see a little farther westwards. A complex of forest-bound hills and spurs pushed in from the north, forcing the river against the steep slopes of the main range, which rose to 12,000 feet. Before us were hints of an expanding vista and of something new to see next day other than fresh stands of timber.

We continued climbing and descending steadily, leaving the deserted clearings behind. In one of the last we stopped at a convenient hut beside the track and brewed up lunch. Ijomba urged us to continue on as he and the carriers sat down to roast their *mbi*, but we did not like the prospect of the party splitting up and could see no strong motive for it. So we had an extended lunch hour while we waited for the Danis to finish.

Not long after lunch we began to see the logic of Ijomba's urgings. He had assessed our fitness and capabilities pretty well and while he and the carriers disappeared rapidly up the next long climb we stumbled and struggled with the worst track we had encountered. It was obviously little used. Numerous fallen trees lay across the track without even native notches to give our boots a grip. It became a purgatory as we stretched across tangles of branches or ducked beneath half-fallen trees: packs became stuck, forcing us down on our knees in the mud to get clear. Then a gash of sticky brown clay was succeeded by a network of slippery roots, until our ears were filled with the noise of our own stertorous breathing and grunts and curses as we dragged our boots from quagmires. Our minds became dulled as we forced our tortuous way upwards; the climb became a nightmare of groping through this never-ending cleft that split the jungle before us.

Dave dropped behind and the rest of us waited, seated on our packs. We chewed a bit of scroggin and silently commiserated with each other, looking at our bedraggled clothes and white, tired faces. Someone murmured a comment on the situation and suddenly without reason we smiled, giggled and were soon crashing into the merciless silence with great uproars of laughter, giving a wide vent to the bottled-up strain and tense effort of the previous hours. This was followed by loud, concerted 'Halloos!' until Dave's faint call came answering back. We started to shiver in the coldness of the forest after twenty minutes' inaction and the sweat was icy on our backs. When Dave arrived we started off immediately to get our stiff limbs into smooth motion, to warm up, to climb and find the sun. We took a few pounds' weight each off Dave to help him keep with us. Duncan, possessed by some sudden spark of energy, bored ahead and after a while we heard his excited 'Yahoo!' above. We followed, to burst into a grassy clearing, where the sudden glare of sun hurt our sweat-ringed eyes.

The carriers were there beside a smouldering fire all asleep and arranged perfectly like the petals of a flower with their feet towards the embers. We woke them with ironic shouts of 'Nawok!' and then flopped down as they stirred, moaning and groaning. The track wound to the crest of a grassy hill. Intent on finding a camp site quickly we soon sped on to get the hilltop view. This showed only a stretch of clearings which thinning forest revealed to be almost flat. We had left the hills for the time being and at the back of my mind the plateau raised its mocking head once more. We tramped down to the perfect site for Camp Four. It was on a dry grassy shelf beside a deep stream. A bank topped by a lone casuarina tree and tussocky flats led towards the river. As we climbed down a bank of clouds to the west cleared away: blue and stark against the evening sky rose an array of fang-peaks. We hoped that they were related to the Carstensz. Even if they were not they gave us inspiration and hope.

There was a noticeable breeze for almost the first time, and its rustle through the casuarina leaves provided welcome company as we cooked up dinner. There was a *kanangda* immediately beneath the tree but before they settled into it the Danis appropriated our ice-axes and disappeared over the bank. This was mystifying and we expected them to bring the axes back gory from the blood of wild pig or perhaps wallaby. Instead they returned with crayfish, which must have made a welcome addition to their steady diet of potato. It was known to us that the Baliem, in fact all highland rivers, were devoid of fish and the crayfish had the water to themselves.

That night was scheduled for our first radio contact with the Government station at Enarotali on the Wissel Lakes. Puttoh walked up a nearby hill to see if it was suitable for stringing up an aerial but decided that although we were fairly high, 8,500 feet, the surrounding hills would effectively restrict the range of our transmitter. So we made no attempt at contact. We had a week's grace in which to begin transmission and were safe from the expense of 'rescue' flights. The Dutch Government had authority to undertake rescue activities only if we failed to contact them within a week of 12th June.

After the ambush near the Pass of Arrows above the Yi Meleri River. The carriers had regained their confidence. *See* page 37. (*P. Temple*)

Tuans clustered round him to photograph his feathers and paint. *See* page 34. (*D. E. Cooper*)

The Danis at play in the Baliem valley. (*P. Temple*)

The compound guarding the Baliem River. More of our carriers arrived.
See page 48. (*D. E. Cooper*)

We felt the all-embracing contentment of warm, comfortable rest after a hard day. With dinner finished before dark we lay in our sleeping-bags in and around the tent and talked as the light failed. The Danis murmured quietly and the fire disappeared into ashes.

I awoke to find the tent roof sagging, damp and yellow, over my nose. As it inched lower I became dimly aware of tent pegs being pulled out. As Duncan shouted 'Get up, you lazy b——!' I realized what was happening. Before he could collapse the tent completely I dived out of my bag with unaccustomed speed and chased him wildly up the bank, over the grass and in and out of the breakfast pots in a vain effort to push him into the stream. He was too wily and I cursed ineffectually, to the merriment of everyone else. It was an invigorating start to a long day.

After a breakfast of porridge and scrambled eggs we climbed the bank and set off across the damp flat towards the next stretch of trees. We went at a good speed, eager to take in the view promised at the next clearing. The belt of forested mud did not last for long and we strode out to see expanding, undulating country clothed in long grass. The complete view was still hidden by a further line of forest and we pressed on to pierce its screen.

Puttoh took one step forward—and the vision of long grass dissolved. He sank to the knees in swamp: the grass was reed. The heaviest member of the party, with probably the heaviest pack, he dragged his boots from the clutching mud while we agonized from *terra firma*. I took a deep breath and looked around for some means of escape but the high thick belt of reeds was an effective barrier. Through it the natives had worn a gap, a track no better than a stream of mud, and this we had to follow. Rather than tempt the maw of the mire in the centre we trod along the track's edge, balancing on the roots of the reeds. Our legs ached at the effort and frequently the reeds would break, subjecting us to the tiring suction and drag. We learned to our cost that if there was any delay in removing one's foot the clutch of the swamp tightened and strengthened with each second. Someone sent up a moaning ditty: 'Mud, mud, glorious mud—there's nothing quite like it for cooling the blood!'

E

We sank exhausted by the next trees and looked upon the moss forest with different eyes. It seemed a haven in the wilderness. When the party was all together again we carried on and passed the trees to another belt of swamp and yet another line of trees. Rather than cross directly to the trees we angled to their northern corner where a small, scrub-covered hill rose out of the reeds. After more of this wading, sucking and dragging our eyes became trained quickly to seek out the drier patches for our weary feet. At the top of the hill we stopped again, having need to find our position. Another basin rolled out to the west. The main range to the south stopped short and its higher continuation lay some miles farther back with a distinct break between. The southern bank of the river lay flat and swampy, then rose in thick forest and scrub to the steep walls of the main divide. There some fine peaks stood clear. High on their flanks, ancient glaciation had carved U-shaped, hanging valleys and smoothed bluffs. On our northern bank the scene undulated between belts of swamp and low spurs sloping gently towards the river. There were clumps of trees among this pale green and brown country but farther to the north more thick forest merged into high, broken hills. Far to the west a range ran at right angles to our path, while in the south-western corner, in the direction of the Carstensz, there was an indistinct jumble of hills and peaks. We were not spared anything: the swamp rolled out before us like a soggy pile carpet. The broad, rocky plateau had been well watered down.

We had a few mouthfuls of scroggin to fortify us. Dave's leg must have suffered badly in the swamp and he endured it stoically. Rather than see him drop behind we split his load among the rest of us. We descended to the next swamp, crossed the next spur, descended to the next swamp, crossed the next spur— continuing thus all day. The only relief was the expanding view and the differing aspects of the rock peaks to our left. These we deduced were part of the Prinz Willem Range, a name scrawled vaguely across one of our unrealistic sketch-maps. They may offer a worth-while objective for an expedition—if the peaks are really limestone and not mud.

Occasionally our path was broken by deep, slow-moving

streams and by one of these we stopped for lunch. It was an early meal because grey clouds were steadily filling the sky. They looked ominously different from earlier banks of cloud, presaging rain. We were all exhausted and wedged ourselves comfortably amongst the steep, dry tussocks of the stream banks. I relaxed completely, not daring to move a muscle. No one stirred unecessarily until Puttoh and Duncan exhorted us to action, then we made a drink and ate a few biscuits. We chewed moodily, glooming over the prospect of an unknown length of swamp to come.

We rose wearily to our feet and edged across an array of logs spanning the stream. Puttoh caused it to creak ominously, but when Dave crossed the handrail collapsed and he had to wade. Even the carriers had lost some of their energy and walked more quietly than before, resting regularly beside the track. It was a morose and grim expedition that trudged mechanically across the Baliem's silent sheath of mud that afternoon.

The country must have looked magnificent from the air, green pastures on gentle hills—ideal for dairy cows, with a gentle, winding river watering its verdant banks. But it was neither thick enough to plough nor thin enough to sail on. It was an unflagging destroyer of energy and will-power, it sapped at the very roots of determination. We rapidly succumbed to the first symptoms of mountaineer's foot—the inability to put one in front of the other —but it was impossible to give in. We seemed to have been led into a well-laid trap. To give up and return meant just as much misery as going on: that fact became the foundation of progress.

We trailed Ijomba, who did not seem to know the meaning of tiredness. We rested on every other spur for five minutes and then that cruel shout of 'Nawok!' pulled us to our feet and over the rise into the next sea of reeds. As I carefully sidled a section of the track Lynn yelled: 'Hold it! I want a photo. Can you move a bit over to the right?' I stepped over to the right and sank gently to my knees. 'That's fine. Carry on!' As I dragged my legs out, the camera clicked over the noisy sucking and my loud abuse: 'I hope the b—— thing's underexposed!'

The rain insinuated its way into the afternoon. Not suddenly or strongly, but gently it fanned out over the landscape, imperceptibly reduced the visibility and quietly began to soak us through. We donned our ponchos for the first time. These were nylon capes with hoods, made especially for the trip; they immediately brightened the scene with their various colours of scarlet, turquoise and black. The rain stopped for a while as if the first showers were just a warning. We saw a little sunlight and were congratulating ourselves on our good luck when the heavens opened and the rain thrashed us along.

On most spurs there were *kanangdas* in various states of disrepair. I looked hopefully at them as possible sites for camp. My queries of 'Nogo?' produced no response from the Danis, who just discussed the situation among themselves and then set off at a trot down the track. Later they fobbed me off with 'Ndanda', and when I began to look more discouraged and bedraggled, 'Awo'. I looked out for every excuse to stop and rest. When the carriers stopped to catch more crayfish I lolled on the bank of the stream and watched as they waded carefully downstream, feeling under the overhanging grass and earth. They had picked that stream out of the several we had passed and, sure enough, they came up grinning with nine crayfish about six to eight inches long. Their *mbi* was running low and we were glad to see them catch this little extra food. Another excuse came for a rest when Dave found a prize example of the bottle plant. He poked holes in the soft, pineapple-shaped fruit and photographed the thousands of ants which poured out to examine the breach.

Eventually the day came to a close—it seemed as if it never would—and I tramped to the camp site in the rearguard with Dave. We crossed the remains of a small village by the edge of the river. Its meanders had thinned considerably and we had no trouble wading through the gentle current to the south bank. Camp was in a comparatively dry hollow by a stream. Around it was burnt-out scrub which blackened everything that touched it. The range we had to cross to Ilaga loomed much closer now, about ten miles away, and we hoped that a day would see us to its foot and two days over to the mission station.

It rained steadily as we cooked our stew on the hissing fire. Sandflies in their thousands swarmed over our bodies and forced a retreat into the tent to arm ourselves with D.D.T. We prepared for a night-long battle, but cold and darkness drove them away.

Getting into the tent without bringing mud on to the ground-sheet became a highly developed art. One had to sit on the edge of the door, half in and half out of the rain, to pull off slimy boots and mud-encased gaiters, which were promptly thrown to a spot where they would be likely to receive a good washing overnight. Parka and trousers were tucked under the tent eaves, followed by a quick, shivering scramble into the warm, dry luxury of down-jacket and sleeping-bag. It was found a less unpleasant process to dry one's shirt on the body in the comfort of a bag than to suffer the clammy horror of its cold wetness at first light.

Wedging my hip into a comfortable position I wrote up my diary that night by the light of a headlamp, while Duncan brought up to date his geological notes. Although during the past two days there had been no rock to chip, the structure of the surround-ing country had provided him with plenty of food for thought, and he was beginning to piece together a clear picture of the east–west structure of the highlands.

The tent roof began to drip from the creases. We were more comfortable in the tent, nevertheless, than Puttoh and Duncan, who had elected to sleep outside and test the efficiency of their sleeping-bag covers. Puttoh's, which was impervious, became drenched in condensation and Duncan's, which was not imper-vious, became drenched in rain.

The next day we began to leave the swamp behind. Following a bleak breakfast we stamped our limbs into life and followed the Danis into the mist. The valley was narrowing rapidly and the belts of swamp became thinner, broken by dry hillocks. We began to see a river with boulders poking through its surface instead of a brown, unfathomable flood. Our spirits brightened with the sun. Its warmth penetrated our damp backs, raising wisps of steam.

We followed the river close to its southern bank, frequently resting to wait for the carriers. Their energy was flagging from the previous heavy day and they took their time on the easy ground, probing the side streams for crayfish. Puttoh became

worried at their lack of *mbi*. Their *jums* were almost empty save
for a few gnarled potatoes; it was incredible that they could
maintain their pace on so small a diet. Although they had existed
for the whole of their life on sweet potato, with occasional forays
into meat at pig feasts, they generally presented fine physiques
without an ounce of flabbiness or pot-belly. But the strain was
beginning to tell and we decided to give them next morning a big
billy of mashed potato (made from our powder), appropriately
sweetened, to boost them over the Ilaga Pass.

Perhaps the worst afflicted was the Pigman's wife. The way
she had kept up with us in her pregnancy, load and all, was outstanding proof of the primitive strength and natural hardihood of
the Dani people. She was a pitiful sight at times, trudging alone
without the help or even moral support of the men. From that
time on we frequently took her load to relieve her straining head
and back. Ijomba was still the leading personality although even
his fire and power had become subdued. He displayed further
marks of his erudition when he produced three readers, stories of
the Bible written in his own language. He read to us modestly
from these pages of twelve lines, but was outdone by one intelli-
gent boy of fourteen who counted one to ten in English!

It was perforce a shorter, easier day since we had neither the
strength to cover such ground as yesterday's nor hope of starting
up towards the pass before dark. As the track became firmer hoof-
marks began to appear, and on one occasion the prints of a large
bird, which must have been left by a cassowary, the large, flight-
less bird of New Guinea. A few swifts swooped around and from
a distance we heard the cooing of doves. We saw little movement
however. One of the Danis, 'Handsome', caused some excitement when he chased after some rustle in the undergrowth, and
had Puttoh splashing across the river with the shotgun in pursuit
of an elusive pig.

We stopped for lunch in a *kanangda* as the rain threatened. We
became anxious at the non-appearance of Tim, who had dropped
behind. We had ominous thoughts of his drowning since he had
announced his intention of taking a dip in the river, but he finally
arrived limping with a twisted ankle—the result of unaccustomed

walking on rocks. The rain was greeted by a round of yawns before we teetered off along the bank once more. Duncan stopped where the bank had collapsed into the river and dug out his unused gold-pan from the bottom of a yellow kit-bag. He knocked away some boulders and earth, washed it, and after some careful swilling held it up for our scrutiny. Much to our delight some specks of gold swam among the gravel. 'Not much, but warrants further prospecting,' pronounced Duncan gravely, stroking the remnants of his goatee beard, which rapidly was becoming lost in the tangle on his cheeks. 'Evidence of metalliferous mineralization.' Anyway it was gold.

The rain poured down in steady sheets. Lynn and I got up some steam to keep warm and left the others behind, accompanied only by the Irishman and Handsome. At the beginning of the track up to the pass we waited for the main party and sheltered under the ponderous drips of a huge tree. The Irishman tried to wheedle a cigarette from me, but remembering our promise to the mission not to encourage bad habits among the Danis, I refused. He retaliated by producing a piece of tobacco leaf from the tip of his *kepewak*. I did not have the heart to refuse him a light and we soon puffed together in concert.

The others approached some distance away, the bright ponchos dipped in and out of the scrub—and then suddenly disappeared. After a few minutes they had not reappeared and the Irishman let out some piercing yells to no effect. We recrossed the river and after a little searching sat down in a *kanangda* out of the rain. A few fresh footprints outside indicated that another native party had recently passed through. The Danis did not seem in the least perturbed at our own party's disappearance and set to lighting a fire, for a quick scraping away of ashes of the centre revealed red embers. We exhorted them to look for the others: 'Tuan Duncan, Tuan Put-toh!' but the Irishman only grew voluble and chewed the remnants of a crayfish. Eventually Handsome trotted off into the rain. After we had resigned ourselves to a hungry night the rest of the party turned up by the river. The Irishman had used sense in stopping where he was. It proved that the river was the last source of running water before the pass.

Puttoh, anxious not to repeat his wet slumber of the previous night, rigged up the plastic fly for the first time alongside the tent. We were able to eat sheltered from the constant rain. Camp Six was unusual in that it was sited on a pebbly and sandy beach as distinct from soggy turf. The roar of the river over boulders brought back memories of stony tracks and scree slides in Wales or the southern Alps, which had become infinitely desirable after the mud.

With the heavy rain and high ridge before us Puttoh still declined to attempt radio contact with Enarotali. In fact we decided virtually there and then to wait until we reached Ilaga. We fell asleep that night entertained by the fireflies, which danced in the tent roof out of the rain.

5

The Pass of Remembrance

The pass was wrapped
In a blanket of mist,
And the rain came again,
And the wind whipped.

WITH an exclamation that sounded something like 'Yayyyy!'
Ijomba thrust the billy of 'sweet potato' back into Puttoh's hands.
One taste of our concoction had been enough for him. We were
thus left with a mound of sweetened mashed potato to supplement
our normal breakfast. We ate it, grateful for the excuse to rest a
little longer before beginning the day's trek.

Great bands of mist and cloud lay swathing the valley to the
east and seemed to promise later a day of clear blue sky. Puttoh
began breakfast before first light in an attempt to get us away early
on the long climb. His energetic example was not followed since
we lay snug in our bags until the last minute. I massaged my limbs
after a night of cramp and brief nightmare before emerging
stiffly into the sharp dampness and misty light. The ritual of
pulling on wet boots and slimy socks had to be endured, warm
toes wriggling in horror against their disgusting grasp. Rubbing
the grit from my bleary eyes and pushing back my matted hair I
looked dimly past Puttoh, placidly stirring the porridge, to the
icy torrent of the river. I remembered without either sadness or
gladness that this would be our last contact with the great Baliem
and turned to look instead at the tangle of hill forest, which
depressed my low spirits even more.

The time came to leave as the Danis meandered slowly towards

us from their *kanangda* across the water, their toes freezing as
they waded. We struck camp. My pack lay full but open, waiting
for the removal of my down jacket. I waited until two or three
'Nawoks!' had passed and then quickly stuffed the haven of
warmth away, swung up the mule, and ambled off the hundred
yards or so to the foot of the climb.

The track was steeper than in any earlier moss forest, but it
served to warm my legs, steam my trousers, and clear the smoke
of a breakfast cigarette from my lungs. We soon swung into the
rhythm of the roots and rapidly gained height. We estimated
Camp Six to have been at 9,000 feet and that day rose another
3,000 feet to reach the highest point of our trip to Ilaga.

The first 1,000 feet were soon behind us; we plodded happily
on as the forest cleared and the sun struck our backs. We followed
a narrow ridge with steep drops on either side into clinging
undergrowth, then the full extent of the Baliem's upper gorge
slowly swung into view. We had originally thought that the
upper reaches of the river flowed across the elusive plateau.
Although there was no sign of that red herring it was obvious
that the Baliem rose from high limestone country to the south of
our position. It seemed possible that a direct route might be
found from the swampy basin of our trek to the Carstensz range,
bypassing the Ilaga valley. We had no wish to bypass the Ilaga
valley that day. The prospect of the mission station with its
unparalleled luxury, its dry shelter and comfort, was too alluring
a goal.

We topped the trees and the whole wide panorama of the
Baliem swept into view. This was too good to miss and we
indulged in a photographic orgy as we sat on our packs and drank
in with one gulp the long miles of the days before. We could see
back to Camp Three, to the junction of the East Baliem and the
Meleri Hills, vague as they were, in the distance. It was a magnificent view of royal blues, subtle greens, black, white and brown,
yet to us insidiously hostile. To the north, olive green crumpled
infinitely; to the south the Prinz Willem peaks had lost their
pre-eminence and presented dull twists of scrubby limestone.

The track had lost none of its muddiness, excelling even itself in wide, sloppy pools and steep, sticky banks. Later in the morning cumulus clouds began to build up, steadily diminishing the sunlight. I slowed down with the increase in height and was soon labouring alone, with Puttoh, Duncan and Lynn yet again up in front. At the comparatively low height it seemed absurd that I could be unacclimatized to the altitude. Yet the three ahead had all been over 14,000 feet before, whereas Tim, Dave and myself, who had not, lagged behind. I panted on as the sky filled grey and the view diminished.

After passing a collapsed *kanangda* on a spongy flat I topped a rise and met a group of Danis bound for the Baliem. There were about a dozen of them, including two sturdy women, and they were armed to the teeth with axes and bows and arrows. We exchanged *koanas* and the familiar flabby handshake and looked back at the Baliem. Miles away near the site of our Camp Five a column of smoke stood out sharply against the still background. The Danis waved at this, discussing it vehemently. Where they stood, on the edge of the pass slopes proper, was a line of 133 white stones running north to south. This was puzzling. I dismissed it as a boundary line between two native territories but later heard that each of the stones represented one life lost in fierce wars that raged just a few years previously. This was the Dani cenotaph, their field of remembrance.

The Danis trotted off down the hill and I turned to finding my friends. It was past noon and lunch time. It was much later, however, before the smoky lunch fire hove in view. It seemed to lie at an unattainable distance. I climbed in regular bursts of twenty steps, rested over the ice-axe, made another twenty steps, rested. . . . At last I flopped down exhausted by the fire and waited patiently until I had strength enough to pour a cup of tea from the billy. Tim, who had arrived just before me, lay flat on his back, immobile, staring at the sky.

Most of the Danis had gone on, their energy renewed with Ilaga in sight. It was not long before Puttoh, Duncan and Lynn got up silently, threw on their packs and grimly marched on. I waited a while longer until Dave arrived and the first spatter of rain fell across my cheeks. My legs wobbled as I pulled on my poncho but soon the invigorating lash of cold water spurred me onward.

The crest of the pass was in sight. The spine of the ridge was now almost bare of trees and the scene was of sodden turf interspersed with patches of gnarled scrub and scattered tarns. All colours were washed out and with the grey flatness of the sky presented a bleak monotone. The wind was almost unhindered and to preserve my last vestige of warmth I had to wear parka as well as poncho. If I expected to meet a striking view on top I was disappointed. There was nothing save windswept, rolling ridge. The rain became heavier and I was overjoyed to see smoke filtering through a bunch of trees. Camp! In my hurry to reach it I ran and fell headlong in the mud, slipping on an incongruous outcrop of rock. My beautiful blue parka was never the same.

It was not camp at all but a shivering group of carriers who were huddled round a miserable heap of logs trying to ward off the rain and smoke. Their sacks and an appropriated poncho were being used as raincoats but they must have felt the cold bitterly. They were better on the move, so vigorously shouting 'Nawok!' I set off again. They began to follow in dribs and drabs. It was not long before I caught up with our little pregnant lady. At the sight of her running nose and look of utter misery I took the *jum* from her and tied it to my pack. My legs almost doubled as I took up the combined load—hers must have been well over thirty pounds. I gritted my teeth and hoped fervently that camp was not much farther. We exchanged wan smiles.

As I tramped into the gathering darkness the familiar figure of Puttoh bulked ahead. 'Camp's not much farther. Beautiful site, soft grass on a flat by a stream.' I carried on, crossed the stream and squelched across the saturated moss of our grassy flat. With a shy *koana* the Pigman's wife took her *jum* and disappeared down the slope towards a *kanangda* in the trees. We dragged up the sodden tent, rigged the fly from the entrance pole and started to pressure-cook our stew. Five of us squeezed into the four-man tent as the rain changed to a fine, enveloping mist. Puttoh was left out in the cold and dark administering to the stew by the light of a headlamp.

Although everything was in a more sodden state than ever we all felt happier: Ijomba had told us that next day we might reach Ilaga if we marched hard. The mist started rivulets down the inside of the tent and the cold struck up through the floor, but nothing discouraged our cheerful banter as we devoured that meal. Through an oversight I had lost my strategic position at the end of the tent out of the drips and slept awkwardly with my head down the slope. I could not sleep for a long time and then it came with a recurrence of horrible nightmares, which had started the previous night.

Fortunately it never rained in the mornings and 16th June was no exception. It was cold, nevertheless, and we stamped our chilled feet as we stuffed saturated sleeping-bags into our packs. The sun was nowhere to be seen despite our height of over 11,000 feet and the cloud effectively insulated us against its heat. We packed up in record time, anxious to warm up and reach the mission that day. The Danis would not budge no matter how loud our 'Nawoks'. I felt impatient and angry as I shivered and waited with stiff pack webbing pushing coldly on my back and no sign of movement from the carriers. Finally Ijomba stood up and pointed to the clouds; hugging himself against the cold, he muttered 'Awo'. They wanted to wait for the sun, so we piled the loads before them and set off with only the Pigman as guide.

The morning revealed a succession of tarn-covered rises and hollows with no intimation of the Ilaga valley until deep side gullies fell away from our line of travel. The silence of the New Guinea highlands was rudely broken by a constant yelping and chattering. At first we attributed this to the carriers but realized that it not only came from behind but from all sides. Nothing stirred, no flock of birds took to the air; we finally put the noise down to frogs.

The cloud dissipated a little and rose higher, revealing a complex of deep valleys running away to the north-west. This country held the source and the tributaries of the great Rouffaer River. Jagged peaks and startling cliffs of limestone loomed through the mists giving a tigerish display of nature in the raw.

We were kept in infuriating suspense. Duncan estimated the mission to be down the valley some hours while I secretly wished and hoped that he was wrong. It was impossible to derive accurate information on times and distances from the Danis, who had no way of figuring either. They divided years, miles, minutes and yards into *awo*, *ndanda* and *paybi* ('soon', 'long way off' and 'long time coming'). It was irritating to be told that Ilaga was *ndanda* since it could mean three hours or three days, so we had to plod from rise to rise in ever repeated disappointment.

I felt indescribably tired and rested with a cigarette while the others went on. It was not long before the carriers caught us up, slipping delicately along the track with kit-bag and sack. I watched their easy, rhythmic movements with envy and followed one with my clodhopping boots in poor imitation.

Towards noon I came to the final crest and stared astonished at an airstrip thousands of feet below and shining in distant sunlight. Metal glinted, and in a wide, cultivated valley wisps of smoke rose up from many villages. I dropped my pack and absorbed the view that we had been awaiting after many weeks of planning. The prospect of a dry bed that night became unbearably tantalizing and I plunged off the top towards the distant haven.

I had gone down a few hundred feet before I realized that boot- or foot-marks on the track had disappeared. Despite the presence of *kanangdas* farther on, I was on the wrong path. Groaning, I regained the unwelcome heights and began combing the multiplicity of tracks for signs of the party. As I was doing so, Dave and Tim arrived; we searched in concert and had yet another look down my track. Eventually, a couple of hundred yards farther to the north, I found Puttoh's boot-print and we descended the right track to a rocky outcrop for lunch. To the north across a deep side valley of the Ilaga an impressive bare peak filled the view as we munched sardines and Weetabix. It swept down to the valley in a razor-sharp ridge, from which tall trees leaned crazily in their effort to keep a foothold on almost bare limestone.

Looking at my watch I saw that it was after 1 p.m. and only five hours remained before darkness. In that time we had to drop over 3,000 feet through tangled forest and tramp up the valley to the mission through a complex of villages. As the trees swallowed us up I jigged downwards like a man possessed, racing against the ragged, grey rainclouds that chased over the landscape from the east. In my mad rush I left Tim and Dave behind and was soon alone among the roots and silence.

I tripped or slipped several times on the constant snares of the track and finally paused breathless to pull on my parka. Rain was falling noisily through the leaves. Between some dead trees I could see far away under the layer of clouds a cave of sunlight. It lit up, not more dark blue hills as I might have expected, but a light green plain that disappeared into the distance. It was the plateau. The stage manager called his cue and the curtain of clouds fell.

The descent seemed interminable. Vertical walls of roots followed one after the other, steep drops that seemed to promise the final jump into open fields ended in short climbs and more drops. In the lower reaches logs increasingly blocked the track, which became a replica of the earlier route in the Baliem. The occasional *kanangdas* were unworthy of note until I tramped into a wide clearing where a large structure confronted a mound of old ashes and an assemblage of stakes bound together with bark. This resembled the fences put around young trees in London parks, but of rougher construction with curls and twists of bark springing from it. The trees around were stripped white. A strange sound like the mewing of a lost kitten hovered near my ear and startled me enough to swing round and seek its origin. But there was nothing in sight, no wildcat or bird. It continued behind me and then vanished into the bushes near some scattered bones. The strange bark symbol, eerie noises and bones were enough for me and I ran off down the track as if the local witch-doctor were hard on my heels.

I learned that my superstitious fears were groundless. The scene had nothing, or little, to do with sorcery. The collection of sticks was a fertility symbol erected on every track leading to villages; the noise came from a frog; the bones were those of a pig.

Three and a half hours after lunch I struggled through a cloud of attacking mosquitoes and thrashed through the last under-growth into a slope of high ferns. A huge tree had been felled conveniently as a track through them and shortly I slid off its end by the first Dani hut. Twilight was not far off but before pressing on I was drawn by the roar of a stream to quench a raging thirst. There had been no opportunity for a drink since breakfast. As I rested for a while I estimated that the others could not be far ahead—I had passed a still bright fire about an hour before on the ridge. Similarly Tim and Dave could not be far behind. The big problem was to find my way through the hills and fences to the mission before nightfall, and *en route* make the crossing of the Ilaga River, which looked twice as violent as the Meleri.

I stumbled through someone's back yard and after climbing a couple of stiles found myself in a large compound. The first thing that took my attention was two large pigs, larger than any we had encountered near Tiom. I stood helplessly in the centre of the compound, trying to define a trail through the jumble of huts and fences that faced me to the south. I felt almost like a stranger to London who, while staying in Croydon, tries without a map to find a street in Hampstead. The mission was hidden behind a steep hill. As the villagers ducked out of their homes and came to examine me, I pointed in its general direction and calling out '*Tuan* Larson'. Gordon Larson was, I knew, the missionary at Ilaga. I had met him briefly at Sentani, and hoped that the magic sound of his name would inspire one of the Danis to lead me to him. But my words seemed only to puzzle them. I was overjoyed to see Handsome and another of our carriers, 'Glum', appear behind the crowd that had gathered. They shouldered their way to the front, handed my pack to a strong teenage boy and instructed him with a string of words punctuated frequently with '*Tuan* Lartar'. I then realized that Larson's name had been corrupted due to the lack of the letter *s* in the Dani language. Before I had time to collect my wits the teenager was off up the valley, closely followed by two smaller boys and Glum.

We scrambled down to a stream and up the other bank. I had a hard time keeping up with the scampering feet. We crossed a high stile and arrived in the next village, where two women came

We woke them with ironic shouts of 'Nawok!' Between Camps 3 and 4 in the valley of the Baliem River. *See* page 50. (*D. E. Cooper*)

Mud, mud, glorious mud! By the edge of the Baliem River. *See* page 51. (*D. E. Cooper*)

Feeling for crayfish under the over-
hanging grass in a tributary of the
Baliem River. *See* page 54.
(*D. E. Cooper*)

The plateau was at last spread out before us. Height 10,500 feet. Carstensz
Range behind. *See* page 100. (*P. Temple*)

out and gave me freshly roasted sweet corn and potatoes. I was starving and gratefully accepted the food, but forgot that a payment or present was expected in return. I chewed off the tasty nodules of corn as everyone watched, waiting for my favourable reaction. After a while two women set up a gabble, obviously at the non-appearance of beads, so that I began to feel a little ashamed and embarrassed and hid the remainder of the food in my pockets. Understandably tongue-tied, I could offer no explanation of my impecuniosity save a profusion of *koanas*, and was thankful when Glum waved me on over the next stile.

Being relieved of my pack made little difference to my performance. I panted up the steep tracks clutching at tufts of grass for help. The Danis regularly drew ahead and waited on the top of stiles with grins until I clambered up to them. The younger boys often ran alongside, their tripping steps contrasting with my steady thump, thump, thump. Glum quietly relieved me of one sweet potato and then took the pack as we approached a wide tributary of the Ilaga River. I was obviously considered incapable of wading safely. They insisted on holding my arms as we crossed the thigh-deep water.

The light was beginning to fail and I breathed a sigh of relief when we crossed a hill to find the mission houses in view on the other side of the river. Glum stopped by a group of pretty girls and said farewell to me, so I continued alone through a crowd of children towards the bridge. The bridge was the most spectacular of the many we had encountered to date, swinging across a dirty white and brown torrent in a complexity of vine cables. The footway was a flat, narrow strip of wood about six inches wide. As I put my clumsy foot on to it the small boy half way across turned round in horror, waved me off and continued carefully on. If he found it risky, how would I find it? It did not prove to be bad save for the usual ice-axe entanglements and I was soon climbing up the western bank into the sunset.

I pushed my way through a throng of chattering Danis and found Puttoh, Duncan and Lynn. Wearing a *petari* (hair-net), fair and bespectacled, Gordon Larson stood discussing the trip with them. I shook hands and renewed our short acquaintance.

F

'You've had a long walk, Mr Temple.'

I was short of breath or I might have replied: 'The under-statement of the year' instead of: 'Yes.'

We stood talking for a while as the night gathered and then with no sign of Tim and Dave we made our way gently up the track towards the silhouette of a half-built house. We were back into the old routine of *koanas* and handshakes as children, fathers and elders lined the track to meet us. White men appearing from the Baliem was quite an event since normally they came by the yellow birds of M.A.F. Our carriers had disappeared, no doubt to friends' and relations' homes for a happy reunion and, above all, for a good feed. They had done their job exceptionally well, taking us from Tiom to Ilaga in seven and a half days without mishap and without squabble. Puttoh recounted details of the triumphant entry to the first villages. Before leaving the forest, Ijomba had borrowed a razor blade and soap and dived into the bushes, to reappear almost clean shaven and washed. Then, suitably groomed, he was prepared to face the music. He was fêted through all the villages and acclaimed for the great scholar and wise man that he was among the Danis. The people's expression of admiration confirmed our silent tribute.

Our immediate problems were food and shelter. Puttoh intended to pitch the tent by the river but Mr Larson would hear none of this and asked us to use the half-completed house. This was wonderful: we would have a roof over our heads and plenty of room to move about in. We were provided with a Tilley lamp, a pail of crystal-clear water and told to make ourselves at home. On instructions from '*Tuan* Lartar' the Danis brought us *jums* full of *mbi*, taro, sweet corn, bananas and sugar cane. Our stock of European food was low. We wanted to conserve this against delay in replenishment and from now onwards switched to a diet of native food.

Each boy who had carried our packs to the mission, each Dani who had brought food or performed a small service, such as carrying water, had to be paid in beads, and Duncan had an unwelcome task amid darkness and deafening noise. The crush was tremendous as he tried to get at the line of little boys and women who held out leaves in their hands. By the waning light of our headlamps it was almost impossible to tell who had been paid and who had not, and I noticed mischievous little grins as someone obviously received double payment. Occasionally the tiny beads were spilled on the rough ground and we felt imploring clutches at our sleeves, dragging us to the scene of disaster with our headlamps. Finally pay hour was over and with roars we chased them away so that we could have our meal in peace.

We stuffed ourselves with the fresh vegetables until we lay sated in our sleeping-bags on the hard but dry floor-boards. Any muddy or wet articles were firmly shut outside or hidden in a corner as we revelled in the feel of dry sawdust and wood shavings. The loud hiss of the Tilley lamp was hardly heard above our untempered laughter and approving belches. A few Danis who had lingered on after nightfall peered through the unglazed windows with grins of perplexity. We felt a great satisfaction, a great relief that the worst of the trek was over. We could look back to the Baliem days almost objectively, our diaries secreting the real story of those miserable ninety miles.

We snuggled down into our bags at the unheard-of hour of ten o'clock. Heavy rain began to rattle on the roof and we suddenly remembered Dave and Tim, who had still not turned up. The thought of an accident dampened our good humour; we had visions of Dave having trouble with his leg, or the two enduring yet another saturated night out. But sleep soon overtook both jokes and anxieties.

6

Ilaga

But why are you leaving, Bill,
When you've just fetched up?
Stay for a bite and a sup
Or a few square meals.

Awaking in partly civilized surroundings, we suddenly realized how dirty and unkempt we were. We had been invited to breakfast at the mission house and with our consciences sparking we galloped down to the river with the community towel and a piece of soap ferreted unexpectedly from a pack. 'Galloped' is a misnomer. Our feet and legs, suspecting no vigorous exercise that day, took the opportunity to rebel and we became acutely aware of all the cuts, bruises, blisters and sores ignored in the activity of the previous week. My legs, in particular, always relax wholeheartedly on rest days and it took conscious effort to stop them bending too much at the knees as I floundered down the steep track.

There was no question of complete immersion in the river. It was too turbulent and too icy for that. But it gave us pleasure to stand with frozen toes in a quiet eddy, washing away the mud, feeling the scratches sting with the cold. While we washed among the boulders the steep bank above was soon lined with curious eyes peering through the bushes on top, anxious to see more of the white man. I pulled on my track suit and climbed back feeling a little more respectable. Tim and Dave were just arriving at the house when we got back and we were glad to see that no misfortune had befallen them. They had not reached the valley before dark the previous night, and after being led from one village to another by hospitable Danis, they elected to stay the night where they were at 11 p.m. They had been given a good feed of pork and slept in a native hut before continuing on that morning.

We arrived for breakfast promptly at 7.30 a.m. Mr Larson's house stood on a prominent shelf overlooking the valley to the east and north. Two-storeyed, it had been built with his own hands and inexperienced native help. It was a wonderful effort for a man with no special carpentry training, and resembled in style, but on a much larger scale, the American log cabin. The beams and supports were of rough-hewn logs and the walls and floor-boards of thick, wide planks. The windows were glazed, mats lay on the unpolished floor, and in the kitchen stood a wood-fired range and kerosene-operated refrigerator. The sight of the latter and of modern furniture seemed to us all the more remarkable when we remembered that every single item had been flown in by the small, single-engined planes of M.A.F. The refrigerator may have just fitted into the baggage space of an aircraft but the range must have been transported in pieces to be assembled by Larson single-handed.

Between the kitchen and the dining-room was a projecting bookshelf and on top of this a large, battery-powered radio transmitter and receiver. The table was set for breakfast. Mrs Larson came forward to meet us as we took off our dirty footwear on the doorstep and we suddenly felt awkward, scruffy and unshaven in the unexpected domestic scene. We sat carefully at table and listened to Mr Larson as he tried to talk above the constant babble from the radio. The latter did give us some insight into the workings of C.A.M.A. and M.A.F. The headquarters of the mission at Sentani talked variously with a mission in the Baliem valley, an aircraft over the Lakesplain, a mission at the Wissel Lakes and with a party in distress south of the Carstensz ranges. That party was typical of many which had set out during previous years to establish the chain of missions across the breadth of Dutch New Guinea. A group of missionaries had travelled to the south of the main divide to establish a station at a centre of unadministered native population. Their task was to select a site for the mission and build an airstrip so that supplies and building materials could be flown in. The party was in trouble, however, since one of its members had suffered a haemorrhage and he lay ill scores of miles from any doctor and in touch with the outer world only by radio. Instructions for his treatment were sent from Sentani and arrangements made with Ilaga to pick up a camp stretcher and a few luxuries for airdropping. From that piece of drama the talk went on to the everyday work of synchronizing aircraft movements and the lines of supply.

Our presence at Ilaga was noted with little demur, though my original letter guaranteeing the expedition's morals and swift passage through the mission was held up as a binding agreement, despite the fact that it was entirely one-sided. We had arrived at Ilaga by force of circumstances and not through a decision to flout the mission's bar—the letter was merely a confirmation of our sincere desire not to hinder any aspect of the mission's vital work. We had arrived on our own weary feet and this, allied with the fact that Mr Larson was not away at the conference, made the C.A.M.A. prohibition of landing at the mission seem pointless— especially when all the pleas, guarantees and explanations were remembered. Our expedition would never have started for the Carstensz had we been ruled by C.A.M.A.'s parochial preoccupations. Although we avoided troubling Mr Larson in every way possible, his hospitality and desire to help pervaded our short two-day stay. Before breakfast Puttoh arranged to talk by radio the next day with M.A.F. on airdrop arrangements.

We got down to the serious business of eating a magnificent American breakfast and soon had tucked under our belts porridge, bacon and eggs, cinnamon rolls and coffee. The Larson children watched slightly astonished as we swept the table bare. A clean, wholesome meal off shining crockery seemed so much easier to eat and digest than a hash from a greasy plastic bowl. As we ate breakfast, we gradually pieced together the story of the Ilaga mission from Mr Larson's conversation and our probing questions. He was the first missionary into the valley in 1954 and had remained there ever since. Coming from New York, his first missionary work was at the station at the Wissel Lakes among the

Moni tribe. In the few years that he spent there he learned their language well enough to compile a dictionary, and was occupied at the time of our visit in compiling a similar one of the Dani tongue. In 1951 Francis Titehalieu, an Ambonese missionary, made a great overland journey from the Wissel Lakes to the Habbema Lake at the head of the East Baliem River and discovered the Ilaga valley on the way. Gordon Larson returned with him later and eventually set up the mission in 1954. Their first experiences were not altogether happy since the Danis attacked them and robbed them of almost all their possessions. But they had hidden away enough trade goods to allow them to buy food on their return journey to the Lakes.

He had a tough and independent people to cope with in the Danis, but their apparently complete conversion to Christianity is proof of his ability and success in his work. He stamped out wars by burning their fetishes and has been able to combine the many hostile factions in the valley into one settled community. The Danis' devotion to a Christian way of life is shown by their regular prayer sessions and the stringent observance of Sunday as a day of rest. No work is done in the fields, not a finger lifted, and it is impossible to buy food on that day. The native's allegiance to 'Tuan Lartar' is manifest throughout the whole valley: he is the focal point of their life, almost the administrative centre for a population of 7,000 people. His influence has banished hate, fear and suspicion, as proven by the friendly and unreserved greetings we encountered everywhere and the happy faces among young and old.

The mission had grown over the seven years of its existence and now he had with him three women as teachers as well as his wife and three children. A second house had been built close behind his own to accommodate the teachers; the half-finished one in which we lodged indicated further expansion. Apart from spreading the Christian way of life among the Danis, Larson had introduced a variety of European vegetables, especially peas, beans, tomatoes and potatoes, all of which seem to thrive amazingly well at 7,000 feet. It had been impossible to do more than this. Many years will pass before the Danis will be induced to suffer the full extent of a European-dominated life. The difficulties of transport will always hinder the valley's development since the problems facing a road builder from the coast are tremendous if not insuperable; nor are the shape and breadth of the valley attractive to the planners of large airfields. The promotion of a well-balanced agriculture and supporting light industries is all that can be hoped for—unless rich mineral deposits are discovered: but Duncan did not hold out much hope in that direction. A monetary economy will be correspondingly slow in arriving since the natives have no one to work for other than the mission and no one to buy their produce. It is a happy state of affairs. The Danis have an abundance of food, an almost disease-free existence, a simple, Christian way of life and none of the accumulating worries of money.

The Danis certainly did not abhor the onset of white civilization, cherishing such improvements as the steel axe over their clumsy stone adzes. The white man's ornaments were much better too, since their colours did not run or fade in the sun and rain. Old tin cans could be used to carry possessions instead of awkward bark purses or hollowed-out gourds; matches, if they could be obtained, were much better than the ancient firestick. Salt was a valued introduction as it was so difficult to obtain by native methods. But perhaps the most valued introduction of all, socially at least, was clothing. The Danis were not naked by choice but by reason of the lack of materials for making clothes— no wool, no animals for skins and no plant for fibres. They had no money to buy clothes, but any clothing the missionaries discarded was immediately pounced upon. Proud was the man who sported shorts instead of a *kepewak*. He was socially superior, a regular playboy, the object of every girl's heart.

After our long breakfast Mr Larson brought out his copies of the aerial survey maps of the area and traced for us his route across the edge of the plateau when he had first reached the valley. The plateau really did exist and my brief glimpse of the day before was confirmed. From his description it seemed as though a mere five days would see us at the foot of the peaks, our elusive mountains on the rim of the day. The maps still did not really make sense as there were no contours and it was impossible to gauge the relative heights of the hills and ranges. The names did not correspond with local designation and knowledge but gave only a bare outline of the country in front of us.

We stepped out into the bright sunshine feeling very contented and very lazy. We pulled on our boots and meandered slowly down the track, over the stile and so to the house, where a substantial crowd had gathered. Our house was being built in the same style as Mr Larson's and was placed similarly on a shelf looking out to the north and east. The valley narrowed to the north before swinging westerly to join up with the Ilorong and eventually the huge Rouffaer River in the Lakesplain. To the east and west the enclosing ridges of the valley rose up to 12,000 feet. The view north-east was dominated by the big, pyramidal rock peak mentioned earlier. We saw that the Ilaga River fell from the south-west, taking hold of numerous tributaries on the way down before reaching the main populated area. The centre of the maze of villages lay immediately below the mission on the wider east bank of the river. From that point the habitations and fields tapered off as the valley narrowed to north and south. Above the cleared line of the fields, heavy forest climbed up to the ridge tops before petering out in the scrubby, tarn-covered country we had traversed. We could not see any indication of the plateau to the south since we were too low and the usual banks of cloud blocked any loophole.

Later in the morning Puttoh and I went up to meet a M.A.F. plane due in from the Wissel Lakes to pick up the airdrop supplies for the sick missionary south of the Carstensz. The airstrip was several hundred feet higher than the mission house and had been cut and levelled from virgin forest. It dropped steeply to the north-east, its boundaries clearly defined by native fences. Puttoh was limping from an infected heel and I was feeling none too bright after heavy sleep, a heavy meal, and in the heavy atmosphere threatening rain. The climb up was exasperating but alleviated by the company of one of the missionary teachers. She took with her a bundle of medicines, tinned fruit and a camp stretcher. These she wrapped tightly in sacks for the airdrop. Our own purpose was to give the pilot letters for Sentani. The Government had become concerned at our lack of radio contact and we had written a note of explanation, intending to make our first attempt to reach Enarotali by radio that evening. Also we had a letter for Mr Steiger, asking him to send us axe-heads for the payment of the second group of carriers we would need to reach the Carstensz. One of the Danis set up a wind-sock and we waited as it hung lifeless in the hot morning air.

The hum from the south-west grew louder and presently a fly of an aircraft crawled across the sky about 2,000 feet above us. It continued down the valley, circled and then aimed for the strip and landed uphill, swinging to a stop right beside us. Chocks of stone were placed beneath the wheels as the propeller spun dizzily to a stop. Hank, a Texan, hopped out to begin unloading. The door was taken off and a surprising array of cargo was pulled out: whole doors, a case of axe-heads, trunks, brooms and carpets. It was all unloaded at lightning speed since the day was drawing on and the weather over the ranges deteriorating rapidly. The airdrop had to be made before it closed up completely. Unloading finished, the door was stowed behind the cabin and the airdrop sacks tied to the floor beside the gap now left in the side of the plane. Hank would have no pusher to help him and besides having to control the aircraft at a low height he would have to push the parcels out. An added difficulty was that Hank had been flying for the M.A.F. for no more than a month and knew nothing of the country he was setting out for. We could feel nothing but admiration as the small plane rose off the end of the strip and, in banking sharply, began to climb inexorably into thick, grey cloud. We heard later that Hank had been completely successful.

We returned to see how the others were faring with the purchase of food for ourselves and the carriers on the final stage of the trek. The scene outside the house was chaotic. Dozens of Danis crowded by every unglazed window and pushed like a sale queue through the half-open door. There was a constant babble as several women with *jums* full of food waited to present their produce to Duncan who, as usual, was the chief buying agent. We managed to squeeze our way in, to be confronted by a great pile of sweet potato and corn. One storeroom of the house was full of it. Everyone wanted beads and the Danis brought anything which might warrant a palm-full. Apart from sweet potato and corn we were offered quantities of every kind of food grown in the valley. One with a huge grin on his face held a large pandanus nut, while another, intent on being Ilaga's first souvenir merchant, brought stone adzes for sale. We could not afford to buy souvenirs at that stage and only wished that the Dutch cents jingling in our pockets were usable in the Dani economy.

Their curiosity was insatiable. They had not come only to sell food but to view strangers. As each woman sold her produce she would not hurry home but linger, adding to the seething throng whose eyes carefully followed our every action. Even our sitting down seemed to be of interest and it was impossible to do anything or be anywhere without scrutiny. I sat at the top of the stairs to be out of sight but it was not long before a black face smiled sheepishly at me from below.

To get away from the clamour I grabbed my dirty clothing and made for a secluded spot by the river to do my washing. I had not gone a hundred yards before a stream of boys was tailing me. One teenager in particular demonstrated that he knew better than I did where to wash. I gave up with a sigh and ploughed across the fields after him. He was right, of course. The section of river-bank we arrived at had a shingly beach and yards of shallow, clear water. With virtually no soap I had to resort to the Indian method of washing and was soon thrashing my clothes furiously against the boulders.

When I arrived back at the house the scene had changed not a whit and Duncan, exasperated, had got to the stage of losing his much-vaunted 'philosophical attitude'. We had enough food and he had the unpleasant task of turning away late-comers. We began hours of continuous shooing but even by nightfall numerous hardy types remained. We were in a truly royal position and began to admire a queen's lifelong patience. Occasionally one of the men would come to us for twine to replace worn-out *kepewak* strings, but the biggest commotion of all was caused by one who sought our services as tailors. His *kepewak* was broken and there was much hilarity as Dave carefully made running repairs with sticky tape.

With the onset of evening we prepared another huge vegetarian meal to appease our unfailing appetites and to replace lost weight. Everyone was noticeably thinner but certainly not ill or haggard. Our beards were sprouting well and their tangles well matched the state of our hair, though not its colour. We all had sore feet and damaged heels where bruising had been caused by the continual suction and drag on our boots. Puttoh, with a double blister, had to endure a painful lancing before he could walk without a hobble.

As the appointed radio schedule hour of 6 p.m. approached, Puttoh busied himself with erecting an aerial from the roof of the house to a nearby tree. The weather looked none too good as billows of black cloud filled the sky with flashes of lightning. Thunder-rain soon began to patter down through a charged atmosphere. After half an hour's work all the radio connections had been made and Puttoh turned the crank handle to test the power output. There was no response. An irreplaceable part had been broken. The instrument that had taken scores of hours to make, that weighed seventeen pounds, that we had carried as a dead-weight all the way from Tiom, that had been one of Puttoh's treasured inventions, was broken. Puttoh thought it had received an overdose of electricity when he first cranked, but more likely heavy handling on the trek had damaged it. His pride and joy was tucked away in a kit-bag and left at the mission. Its loss meant no radio contact on the most important part of our journey, and that we would have to rely entirely on our own devices in the event of airdrop failure, lack of food or injury. It was, on the other hand, a blessing in disguise since it cut seventeen pounds off the total load, and we would not now be plagued by its tantrums and the necessity to keep a strict radio schedule.

That evening we were treated to a striking sunset, all the more appreciated because of the dearth on previous rain-washed twilights. The clouds lifted to the north-west and their greyness dreamed in the reflection of yellow sunlight. A long roller of mist curved sinuously in the black lower valley, and above, silhouetted against a dark blue sky, stretched a stark line of pinnacles. These were a great surprise and there was a scramble for cameras to record the discovery. In the depths of the valley there was no twinkle of light but only scattered wraiths of smoke where the Danis had lit their fires for the long twelve-hour night. We could imagine their ritual as they huddled round the flaming logs in a blanket of smoke, chattering and gossiping, roasting *mbi*, talk subsiding into fitful sleep until the clouded light of another day roused them to tend the fields, visit friends or perhaps finish a job for '*Tuan* Lartar'. They had nothing approaching a semblance of ordered time, being unable to see beyond a handful of dark nights. Tomorrow was far enough away for them since they had no annual festivals, birthdays or holidays to look forward to.

'Sinbad', the boy who had been told by Mr Larson to look after the house, was curled quietly in a corner watching us with untiring eyes. He wore a brightly speckled tea cosy for a hat and this, like a turban, coupled with his light, coffee-coloured skin, rounded face and limbs and impassive expression, made him more suited to an Arabian fantasy than the Ilaga valley. He always bore himself with a quiet air of superiority and could never be hustled or dismayed.

With pencil and carbon paper borrowed from the mission I scribbled out articles for the New Zealand newspapers, trying within the short space of 1,200 words to do justice to the multitude of impressions recorded in my diary since leaving Hollandia. It gave me a chance to gather my thoughts together and summarize our efforts to date. As I wrote it began to rain, our eternal accompaniment, and a wind rose to whip it through the windows and spatter the floor. A light rumble of thunder drummed us to sleep.

The next day was Sunday, 18th June, our second and last day at the mission before setting off for the Carstensz. We would have left that morning had it not been for the Danis' insistent observance of Sunday as a day of rest. Buying our food supplies on the Saturday had been a good move, for they would never have dug ground and carried supplies to us on the sabbath. This did not prevent them from coming to see us, however, and from early morning on we had to endure their curiosity.

Puttoh talked with M.A.F. over the radio at 7.30 a.m. The news he brought back was not good. He had been informed that due to the pressure of forthcoming conference work M.A.F. would be unable to make our airdrops. In fact the real ferrying work to the conference centre in the Baliem was to be done at exactly the time we required our main drop. Larson would be flying out only a day or two after our departure. This was grim news and put the whole success of the expedition in jeopardy. Our only alternative was to hand over the airdropping to De Kroonduif; it was a case of that or abandon the expedition there and then. M.A.F. could not even spare the time to fly extra supplies or axe-heads into Ilaga. There was no other concern flying light aircraft that we could call on for help. We were all a bit down in the mouth as we silently figured the chances of successful drops from Kroonduif's twin-engined Dakotas. Our supplies had been packed for dropping from only fifteen feet above the ground and it was easy to visualize splintered cases and punctured tins after a free fall from 200 to 300 feet. With no radio to guide the pilot we had doubts of their finding us as efficiently as M.A.F. But nothing could be done to better the situation: we had to like it or lump it.

With the now distinct possibility of an airdrop failure we had to rearrange our plans accordingly. We had not enough European food to last more than six days and not enough equipment to allow more than one rope of two men to attempt a climb. To ease the food shortage we had already bought *mbi*, *taro* and sweet corn sufficient for a five-day march-in with a quantity for use at Base Camp. The European food, it was decided, should be used only for climbing or reconnaissance parties while a *blik* (thirty-six pounds) of rice was bought from the mission for emergencies and to bolster our normal diet. Other supplies could not be added so easily. Candles and soap were now non-existent and one essential commodity, toilet-paper, was rapidly running out. It was only a matter of days before we resorted to moss!

Our medical supplies were not plentiful since there had been a great run on plaster, bandages and aspirins both for ourselves and the carriers. We could only hope that no one suffered serious injury. For illness we still had an untouched stock of antibiotics and drugs. Tents were by no means profuse and would pose a problem if we had to split into three separate parties for reconnaissance. It was hardly a promising prospect but there was no question of turning back and we had no time to wait.

The rest of the morning was spent in writing final letters, mending clothes, sorting equipment and silently ruminating over the future. The heel of my boot had been partially pulled away by the suction of mud and I had a busy time repairing it with a pen-knife, neatly slicing my finger in the process. There was blood everywhere and I spent the following days nursing it against knocks—and that was a hopeless task in the forest.

We were invited to attend a service at midday for the ordaining of six Dani preachers. Well before that time we could hear steady chanting from the direction of the mission house and the meeting sounded more like a tribal dance than a church service. It was with some curiosity that we breasted the rise by the mission and looked down at the compound below. On either side of the compound were two large huts, one of which served as a church though it was devoid of seating, decoration or altar. In the centre of the compound a circle of Danis was dancing in and out displaying a sway of feathers and painted faces while they chanted a monotonous dirge, which had no variety of melody or verse. From one side a phalanx of dancers about three deep surged forward from a mound to the edge of the circle as it expanded and then back as it contracted—as if repulsed. The second group sang certain choruses of the chant that gave a powerful synthesis to the whole spectacle. It appeared a symbolic dance to me and I felt that the central circle, representing good, expanded to ward off the phalanx of evil. Larson, however, said that it was a common dance form and represented nothing more than a foxtrot.

As the time for the ceremony drew near, people began to arrive in scores from every direction, all dressed in their best *kepewaks*, beads and feathers. Older chiefs arrived liberally daubed in paint and greeted each other with vigorous displays of finger-pulling. Old friends among the Dani tribe do not use a simple handshake but link index fingers, pull them apart sharply and continue to do so for some minutes until an adequate show of friendship has been effected. The compound rapidly filled up and when Mr Larson came out to conduct the ceremony there must have been several hundred squatting on the ground: a more impressive congregation than most churches obtain on a Sunday in so-called 'civilized' lands.

We chose good vantage points among the congregation while Mr Larson and his wife made their way to the centre of the crowd and began the service. There was no form to the service, no period of hymns and no sermon. Larson merely read briefly from the Bible in his hand, talked to them about the purpose of the ceremony and then handed over proceedings to the elders. Then arose some vociferous argument amongst the Dani hierarchy, with Ijomba and the future headman of our second line of carriers taking a leading part. It appeared that there was a case of adultery to be settled. Some years ago one of the men to be ordained had been accused of infidelity and the moral issues had to be ironed out before the ceremony could proceed. After various speakers had said their piece, Larson stood up; deftly handling all inter-jections, he obviously came up with the correct solution and the ordaining proceeded. It began to rain half an hour after the start of the ceremony. Pandanus leaf raincoats were hoisted over bare heads but the muttering increased as the rain strengthened. It progressed to a downpour. The Danis scattered to nearby huts, there to await drier times for their protestation of faith.

The ceremony lasted two hours before the crowd dispersed, some to a pig feast on the other side of the valley while a few remained to continue dancing. At the end we had to make an offering, and being forewarned we were able to place our presents of *mbi* on the growing pile of food. It was not clear who received this food but it was probably made over to the elders and senior preachers.

We had one major task to perform that day—hire carriers. There was the usual crowd of well-wishers at the house when we returned and with Mr Larson's invaluable help it was not long before we had secured eighteen. This number had diminished to fourteen by the following morning but at least we had sufficient for the journey. It took some time to explain our destination to the Danis since the mountains normally have no interest for them. With Mr Larson's help the word for mountains was finally found, and they began to talk among themselves of the *dugundugoo*. They even understood our demonstration of the Noordwand and we felt confident that they knew where they were going even if we did not.

The payment for the trek to the mountains was one axe-head per man. Since none were flown in for us before we left the area, Mr Larson eventually had to make payments from his own stock of heads and we reimbursed him with a boxful bought in Hollandia on our return. A journey to the plateau was unusual for the Danis since its only attraction was ant-eaters, which they hunted at certain times of the year. Mr Larson had a beautiful skin on the wall of his living-room, but we, running true to form, saw neither hide nor hair of them in our travels. To the east of the Carstensz there is a pass occasionally taken by trading parties from Ilaga to the villages of the southern jungles. The plateau's height and cold were apparently a strong deterrent to regular visits.

The Danis still thronged around the house, infiltrating continually into the rooms, and we fervently looked forward to the release that the morning would bring. One woman brought her albino baby along, and although some New Guinea tribes treat albinos as sacred, here it was one of the crowd. I felt very sorry for the weakling as it lay in its mother's arms with dead-white, freckled skin, white hair and pink eyes. The mud and dirt, which on the normal Dani child was partly concealed by the colour of its skin, showed plainly and gave it a squalid, sickly appearance.

During the afternoon a M.A.F. plane arrived, took away our mail and deposited Francis Titehalieu, who had come to stand in at the mission while Larson was away. He moved into a hut beside our house and we gleaned from him a little of his experiences when he first discovered the valley; but his modesty forbade any lengthy discussion on what must have been a truly epic journey. His hut gave him a measure of privacy from the

G

ever-present Danis. At our own, our theme song had become 'Close the Door, They're Coming in the Window!'

We were ready to go back to the hills. Our little supply of surplus gear, the radio, shotgun and revolver were bundled in a sack and left at the mission. Our packs were prepared, boots greased and carrier loads almost ready. The sky cleared at the cool of evening and by nightfall was packed with stars, presaging a good start to the final stage of our trek.

7

Across the Zenggilorong

Sullen dark bush lies over
The upper reaches,
Thick as a nigger's head
In the coloured pictures
—And no scrub for a bed.

My DIARY for Monday, 19th June, begins simply: 'So we
dried out just to get wet again!' Sunshine poured into the house
early in the morning. We roused ourselves to pull on boots and
walking clothes, but this was no beneficent smile of sunlight—it
was a huge grin, a chortle of sardonic merriment, which meant
goodbye.

We were up early, but hours of wrangling, jostling, arguing
and repacking were necessary before we were free to shoulder our
packs and walk up to the mission to bid Mr Larson farewell. It
was hot and sticky, and although our packs weighed only thirty
pounds they did nothing to help our mood of irritation and
lethargy. Our *au revoirs* were brief but heartfelt. Then we swung
over the first stile and set off southwards. Although only fourteen
carriers were recruited to accompany us to the mountains we
were trailed by a procession of youngsters, women and a motley
of camp followers. They caused a disorganized jumble as we
plodded through the villages in the upper valley, but we made use
of them—for a few beads they carried our packs.

We did not cross the river but traversed high on the western
bank, steadily leaving its roar behind, inexorably approaching the
fastnesses of the moss forest. At first we tramped across fields,
over fences and through villages where crowds lined both sides

of the path to proffer a handshake and *koanas*. We were celebrities
in the valley and everyone wanted to make sure of sighting us.
Now and then someone would inquire of our destination and
when we answered 'Dugundugoo' we received either a blank
stare or a faint smile of half comprehension.

Our new set of carriers did not impress us as having as much
intelligence and discipline as Ijomba's men. On these first days
their helplessness and whines exasperated us. They lacked a strong
headman; their leader, although a preacher, did little to assert his
authority. In fact we never learnt his name, which says nothing
for his personality. The majority were to us nameless, but two
became prominent: 'The Old Codger,' who was amusing when
not infuriating, and 'One-Eye', who proved himself a sterling
character.

We stopped only an hour after leaving the mission to buy
raincoats. The carriers were adamant that we make this purchase
and we rested in the shade while enough were procured from
neighbouring huts. These were made from wide pandanus leaves
and shaped to cover and to be supported by the head, so that they
lay comfortably on the back, extending over the buttocks. We
had left our ponchos with our surplus gear, anticipating less rainfall in the high country, but should have taken note of the natives'
precaution. We slowly got under way again and descended to a
wide tributary of the Ilaga River.

The bush began to thicken, the valley became steeper and
settlement steadily diminished. It was almost midday and towering banks of cumulus began to threaten the sunlight. Our boots
were already thickly caked in mud when we trailed through the
last village. Making for the line of forest, we were confronted by
a fantastic jumble of logs smothered in secondary scrub growth.
The Danis were attempting to expand their fields and had felled
the forest haphazardly so that the ground was covered in scores
of logs up to a hundred feet long lying at all angles and heights.
Isolated trees still stood among a wilderness of stumps; bushes
sprang up in their newly found freedom; new fields had been
fenced out and planted with sweet potatoes regardless of stumps
and roots. The track continued along the logs and we had a

nerve-racking time pulling ourselves up and walking the greasy gangways. Some were wide with thick bushes to hold for support but others were steep and narrow, offering a twenty-foot fall into the mat of leaves should a foot slip off the widely spaced notches. It was not the place to meet anyone coming the other way, but we did: a shy little lady trotted unconcernedly up a sagging trunk towards us. I sidestepped her, expertly I thought, until I found myself swaying stiffly from side to side, arms outstretched like a tightrope walker, before making a series of wild strides to a point of comparative safety, where I lovingly clutched a branch. We weathered the logs with only barked shins and waded a cold, grasping stream to the wall of trees on the other side.

We struggled into the moss forest once more, into the green gloom and the rampage of roots. Thorns found us for the first time, snatching at our hands and arms as we climbed awkward steps in the track. At first the belts of trees were interspersed with open, scrubby clearings and it was not until the second day that the forest enveloped us. We encountered the first clearing at lunch time and climbed up gentle slopes to its head, where we had a bite to eat. That point was the official boundary of the villages. A fertility symbol stood where the track emerged from the upper belt of trees, the track itself being crossed by broken twigs and leaves, which we learned served a similar purpose. Our accompaniment of women and boys left us after a palmful of beads all round and we moved on, our last link with Ilaga severed.

The humidity rose and the sky settled into greyness as the afternoon wore on. It was not long before a warning patter rattled the leaves and we stowed our parkas in a handy position, wary of the sudden downpour. All the same, it caught us as we slid across a wet, sandstone outcrop: an unmitigated thrashing of water. I pulled on my ventile parka for its baptism without the additional cover of a poncho and was soon sopping wet about the shoulders and arms; its ventilation qualities were just too superb.

The rain was the halt signal for the carriers and at the next skeleton of a *kanangda* they stopped for the night. No more miserable contrast with Ilaga could have been found. From the sunny dryness of our house we had willingly moved on to a saturated, unwanted, unheard-of corner of moss forest. The carriers' *kanangda* was only an excuse for one and they had to resort to roofing it with pandanus coats to counter the furious barrage of rain. They moaned and groaned so much that we began seriously to fear their unrest thus early in the journey. There were obvious indications that some wished to return home there and then, axe-head or no axe-head. It was only deft cajolery on Duncan's part and a sudden burst of inspiration from their head-man that kept them with us. Though they returned to their shelter and occupied themselves with fire and food no one could vouch for their inclination at dawn after a wet and icy night. We were more than a little anxious as we pulled up the tent, stretched the fly from a fallen tree and roasted our supper on embers hissing in the rain. If the carriers did leave us our chances of restarting with a fresh team were almost nil: the chief recruiting agent at Ilaga, Larson, would be gone.

How the view of the world changes when camp is set up, stomachs are full and hips are wedged comfortably into a warm sleeping-bag! Our down jackets yet again proved to be an unfailing solace in our sodden state. I lay in my usual end-of-tent position, swaddled in a jacket that bore the name 'Hillary' on the tag and, I hoped, a little luck. I sucked at a cigarette and reflected once more on airdrop possibilities. The attempt was scheduled for the 27th, a Tuesday, little more than a week away, and that evening we had sampled our first full meal of the *mbi* and corn that must last us till then. Apart from the technical prospects of the drop there was the prospect of stomaching *mbi* continuously for a week. We found sweet potato palatable in small doses and Duncan professed to enjoy it, though how much was true enjoyment and how much was a product of 'the philosophical attitude' was hard to decide. Even Duncan must admit that it was a monotonous diet and not one calculated to foster a reserve of stamina or inspire bursts of energy. There were two types of sweet potato, thin with yellowish skins and interior, and fat with whitish skins and interior. The thin ones tended to be tough and stringy but had a more definite flavour than the fat, which were soft and floury. We discovered two ways to cook them: by the native method of roasting them whole, or by pressure-cooking them, skins and all, into a sloppy mash. Attempts were made to vary this menu, but no matter how much soup, rice or spices were added there was the inevitable mush to swallow. We could afford to sneak a limited quantity of food from our European supply, and a typical menu of the march-in was:

> Chicken Soup with rice *à la* Crawford
> *Specialité de* Puttoh, *mbi de Nouveau Guinea*
> Corn *du Feu*
> *Thé de* Ceylon (*sans lait*)

We looked forward to our evening meals with increasing fervour.

Breakfast was generally a messy meal, and the following morning it lived up to its reputation as we stumbled around in pools of water in clammy clothes fossicking for bowls and spoons lost in the mud. That morning we went to the extent of scrambled egg as well as *mbi* to boost our flagging morale, but there was little we could do to raise the carriers' morale, which had sunk to an all-time low. They grumbled ominously and we received a sudden shock when three detached themselves from the huddle at the *kanangda* and made off towards Ilaga with the party's only axe. With agonized shouts of 'The Axe!' we raced off and rounded them up. But they were intent on returning home, and in order to keep the axe we were forced to hire it for the trip by a payment from our dwindling supply of beads. Our own small tomahawk had mysteriously disappeared at Ilaga, and if this one native axe had gone home both the carriers and ourselves would have been severely handicapped in fire-making.

Then there were eleven carriers. If any more had followed the deserters' example we would have been in sorry state. The lure of a new axe-head must have been sufficient to entice the rest on into more rain and cold, for they remained, though complaining and stamping around in the bone-chilling mist. It was not easy to get them moving, and while I set off to warm up my sore feet Duncan stood over them exhorting and cursing. One could not help pitying them in their naked, shivering state. They crouched

over a miserable fire, which generated more smoke than heat,
looking at us with doleful eyes pleading for warmth. They felt as
many a mountaineer has, sitting in the pre-dawn chill, waiting for
the sun to come up, but similarly the cure for a frozen body was
not prayer but movement and a brisk tramp. As I stepped slowly
down to cross a deep gully, Duncan's voice came muffled through
the leaves: 'Nawok! Nawok! Come on you lazy b——! Nawok!'

I walked alone for some time, building up my speed slowly and
letting the heat accumulate comfortably beneath my cotton shirt.
It was refreshing to be alone once more after the Ilaga hustle. I
suddenly had time to think in silent surroundings instead of being
employed in the noise and problems of organization or in the
headlong rush for the next camp. I took a fresh look at the forest
which tumbled around me in its decadent beauty. There was no
burst of life, opening buds or splash of flowers to offset the chaotic
evergreen. It seemed the relic of a lost age before the renewal of
life, sound and movement. The trees were fighting the primitive
battle for existence; a balance of growth had not been achieved
and no room made among the grim twine of roots for anything
other than the original contestants.

Like many others before me I tried to fathom the reasons for
seeking out such remote, inhospitable corners of the world. But I
stumbled inevitably at the barrier of incomplete human knowledge, offering myself the tame answers of the magnet of mountains and man's constant discontent with his environment. It
seemed a long, disconnected way from scrambling on the cliffs at
Scarborough in Yorkshire, cycling a hundred miles in one day
across the Chiltern Hills or sailing the winding waters of the
Norfolk Broads; yet perhaps these had been a prescribed preparation for longer, more unknown journeys. Perhaps this
journey too was a preparation for something greater—though all
were part of the long quest for self-discovery and attainment that
might never reach an end. It was an intriguing though disquieting
thought. Like Ulysses, I was not content with my kingdom.

The scuffle and squelch of boots quickly disturbed my reverie
as the others came down the track. The track made heavy demands
on energy. It dropped to the north-eastward-running tributaries

of the Ilaga, invariably taking the shortest line of descent and ascent regardless of steepness or difficulty. We were high above the river on the western bank and occasionally saw the crest of the ridge to our right. One section of the track had collapsed and we had almost to resort to stepcutting in the clay to get past.

Our pace improved across several sandstone clearings, but the sustaining effects of *mbi* were not far-reaching and by mid morning we had slowed down noticeably. An early lunch was called for and we stopped before midday to force down a big mash of potato. I succeeded in cutting another finger in its preparation and went to the top of the party casualty list with two bandages. Lynn displayed his heel for a fresh piece of plaster and it was not long before some of the Danis came for similar treatment. We plastered up one or two sores, but when the Old Codger thrust forward his hand with a slight scratch it brought forth hoots of abuse and laughter from carriers and *tuans* alike. We gave him an aspirin to soothe his wounds.

Another type of clearing appeared during the afternoon, formed not by hard, rocky outcrops but by the death of acres of trees. There were no signs of burning (which is hardly possible in the climate) and the tree appeared to have suffered a mysterious blight. It was in one of these clearings that I rested while Puttoh, Duncan and Lynn pushed on. It was getting close to rain time and when I neared the next gully of trees drops splashed across my cheek. I made a dive for a collapsed *kanangda* and pulled on my parka while the initial downpour battered the roof. I waited until the first storm had passed and then slid into a narrow path like a defile through particularly thick undergrowth. It descended deeper into mossy tunnels and it was here that my stomach chose to revolt against the change to a *mbi* diet. I sank exhausted on the moss as I fought a losing battle and rested for an age until my legs felt strong enough to meet the next climb. When I cupped my hands to gather water from a little stream I discovered that leeches, black and bloated, were firmly entrenched between my fingers. This was an excuse to smoke a cigarette, and as soon as I lit up I had great delight in burning the revolting creatures from their meal. This proved to be the only section of track where we

encountered leeches. It is hard to understand why they should
have been such an isolated phenomenon.

A half-hour's slow tramp across log causeways and mud
brought me close to camp. Two Danis rushed back down the
track to help Tim, Dave and me. Soon we looked thankfully upon
the sagging yellow of our tent and Puttoh busily cooking dinner
on a smoky fire. It was still raining so I wedged myself under the
fly with the others and gratefully accepted a roasted corn-cob.
The Danis had a good *kanangda* on the other side of the track,
below us, but a few were gathered around our fire and even went
to the extent of tending our billies and pressure-cooker. The
cooker was inadvertently tipped, letting out a loud hiss of steam,
and the circle of Danis shot out from the fireside as if a bomb had
exploded. There were shouts of amazement, half-hearted laughter
and apprehensive glances at the silver pot before they settled down
again.

Tim and Dave came in later. On their arrival we hoed into as
much *mbi* as we could take. Puttoh's principle was that we should
stuff down as much as possible in an effort to equal the calorific
value of more concentrated European foodstuffs. This was an
excellent principle if our throats and stomachs could stand up to
it, but more often than not one plateful was enough. 'Marvellous
stuff!' Duncan would exclaim through a mouthful of potato but
his raptures raised little agrement. The diet was rapidly beginning
to pall. In an effort to improve the taste of *mbi* I took to imagining
my favourite foods as I swallowed, and that combined with fast
eating helped for some days.

The sleeping pattern in camp was now well established. In the
four-man Meade tent slept Dave, Tim, Lynn and myself in that
order from the door inwards—the pattern based on the frequency
with which each found it necessary to relieve himself during the
night. As that implies, I slept like a log and the others expressed
continued amazement at the lack of movement or sound from me
at night. Dave, on the other hand, enjoyed the damp night air and
his regular walks took the place of a camp patrol. The stoics,
Puttoh and Duncan, preferred the wide open spaces of the fly and
paid for their fresh-air addiction by being continually wet. On

that night the tent promised to become overcrowded as a few black faces peered hopefully at us coddled in our sleeping-bags. Like the crowds at the house in Ilaga, the Danis imperceptibly infiltrated into the tent and began to make themselves comfortable by the doorway. This had happened the night before when one of the teenage boys had wrapped himself in Dave's parka and spent a considerably drier night than his elders. We allowed him in again but shooed away the rest, including the Old Codger.

We struck Camp Ten the next morning at the unusually late hour of 7.45 a.m. The moss forest seemed to be enfolding us in its deathly grip. We lacked both the will and the energy to make an early move. While we grimly chewed our potatoes for breakfast a delegation arrived from the Danis. They remonstrated against our eating *mbi*, evidently under the impression that we were devouring their own supplies. They were very agitated and Duncan had laboriously to discuss with them the question of food supplies and cache a dump of *mbi* for them to pick up on the return journey. They still looked wonderingly at the comparatively small bags of food and were obviously at a loss to understand how we should exist in the *dugundugoo*. We all imitated aeroplanes with our hands and a chorus of engine notes sounded noisily, punctuated by dull 'plops' meant to indicate a package being airdropped. They watched our little pantomime with an expression that said, 'Wonders never cease!'

I left early again to test my feet and stomach and found that the initial steep climb put me into fine fettle once more. I moved at a surprising pace and it was not until I stopped two hours later that the others caught me up. The indications were that we were approaching a pass at the head of the Ilaga valley, but it was impossible to estimate whether it would take us direct to the plateau or into more forested valleys. We were now much nearer to the high ridge on the eastern side of the Ilaga and were reaching a point close to the river's source. The first hour of the morning called for a very steep climb into the open ridge-tops. This done I was soon walking along the crest of a high ridge or spur, the summit of which proved to be the pass. The ridge was not clear enough to permit a view and I had to content myself with intricate manœuvres to avoid wide ponds and mudpools that were littered across the track. On rounding a corner I was much surprised to be confronted by two Danis walking slowly towards me. Their shock at seeing a white man was well blanketed by their hunger, which they ably demonstrated with open mouths and imploring hands. They had obviously come a long way, probably from a village in the southern jungles and over the pass near the Carstensz. I pointed behind me, assuring them with 'Awo', and they continued on to meet their kinsfolk.

From that point the track fell into almost completely clear country. At a prominent point lower down I waited for the others and morning tea. 'Morning tea' by this stage was only a figure of speech since our supply of tea had almost given out and we were saving the little remaining for the mountains. Nevertheless we had some Andrews Liver Salts and this fizzy drink did much to quench my thirst. My 'tea biscuits' were a brace of vitamin pills.

The view raised our spirits since it gave us some idea of where we were going. We had left the Ilaga behind and the track had swung round to run due west. It was enclosed to the north and south by steep, scrub-adorned ridges, which displayed occasional outcrops of white limestone. In the distance lay a jumble of blue-black hills, while immediately below us and stretching to the middle distance was a clear, flat shelf which ended abruptly at the edge of a deeply incised valley. The limestone outcrops and thinning vegetation seemed a portent of the plateau, though an actual view was still denied us. Duncan sat on a rock busily bringing his notebook up to date. All the way from Tiom he had made careful sketch-maps and notes of our route, filling in geological details.

We trotted down briskly to the flat to find it still another stretch of swamp. It was undrained—a high shelf layered with mud. At its beginning there were two or three burnt-out *kanang-das* and at one of these the Danis stopped to roast potatoes. We pushed on farther and halted at the edge where the track plunged down into the forest. After much delay we persuaded some wood to burn and began a protracted lunch hour, bathing in a much appreciated hot sun. The carriers arrived shortly afterwards, at the same time as another group of Danis who were heading for Ilaga. After *koanas* were exchanged an axe was offered for sale at the cheap price of a few shells. We gratefully accepted. This would enable us to keep an axe while the carriers had theirs for the trip back. After they had gone One-Eye came to us for the new axe. We directed him to use the old one in the carriers' possession. He shook his head, indicating that there was no other axe. With a little investigation we realized that we had been 'done'. The travelling salesman had cunningly sold to us the axe we already possessed. How it had been managed with or without our men's connivance was a mystery, but we decided to keep the axe for ourselves as punishment for an act of dishonesty.

The headman came to us while we finished lunch and issued a warning on the river crossing to come, suggesting that we would need the Danis' help. My stomach turned over gently. There is nothing I abhor more than a dangerous river crossing, and the fact that a warning had been necessary meant it would be just that. We opened out our aerial survey maps to pinpoint the big river, which apparently lay below us over the edge of the flat. We guessed it was the Zenggilorong, which rose on the plateau, an important feeder of the Ilorong and subsequently the Rouffaer. I straightened up and listened carefully, but could hear nothing of its roar; only the deep gorge suggested its power.

The track fell very steeply, so steeply that many parts had been washed away or formed the 'V' bed of streams. Newly fallen trees were a problem. At one point the bared roots of a tree above us projected chest high in our path. As we rapidly lost height the noise of the river increased from a faint rumble to a steady roar and the distant sound of waves flooding against its bank warned us of its size. I took my time, not wishing to come to grips with the river before it was absolutely necessary, but it was not long before the bushes parted and a mass of water swept across our path. Stepping to the water's edge, I swallowed hard when I saw that the only means of crossing lay over a slimy, moss-fringed log rising gently to the other bank about a hundred feet away. The river was in a gorge, not a typical gorge of high, restricting rock-walls, but one formed by the tenacity of the moss forest, holding the vertical banks firm against any encroachment by the water. The dirty, boulder-strewn river tore sharply round a bend to our left, rushed straight past us and swung round another boiling bend to the west. Logs sailed quickly past, diving over the short drop in the river immediately below the 'bridge'. We shouted heartening comments at each other above the deafening noise, watching carefully as the Danis walked steadily across with their feet spread outwards and their toes tenaciously gripping the slippery surface. If anyone fell in there was no chance of rescue.

With that fact uncomfortably prominent in my thoughts I tucked in behind Puttoh as he pulled himself on to the end of the log. The first part was easy. I gained confidence, but the grip of my rubber boots depended entirely on perfect balance. The crucial part lay almost half way across where the log narrowed and then rose more definitely to the top of the opposite bank. When I reached this point Puttoh was striding quickly off the end and the bounce of his fourteen stone made the log shudder. My foot slid to one side and suddenly I was on the point of unbalance. My eyes dropped to the offending foot and were immediately caught by the hypnotizing rush of water below. It took a conscious effort to drag my stare away and focus it rigidly on the bank ahead. Gingerly I continued on and then, with my footsteps growing firmer, I dashed off the end and took firm hold of a root. I pulled myself up and leaned heavily against a tree, my strength suddenly spent.

Only Dave remained and we waited until he appeared at the edge of the track and made to cross. He started for the log without taking the precaution of washing the mud from his boots, and we bellowed ourselves hoarse until he heard and understood our instructions. Then he was with us and no time was wasted in pushing on away from the worst obstacle we had met in our travels.

We entered another sandstone clearing and began to climb sharply to the south, almost parallel with the course of the river. The rains came as we pushed through trees to a higher clearing, where the track swung westwards once more. We could sense that we were on the very brink of the plateau. The ridge top before us displayed a clear edge rather than a rolling crest and the forest was unmistakably at its upper limit. Our hope of seeing it that afternoon was squashed when the carriers stopped at a long, well-appointed *kanangda*. This was by far the best we had seen and seemed to signify an important stopping point. Two fires could be accommodated beneath its roof, and while the carriers warmed themselves at one end we enjoyed the luxury of cooking under cover at the other.

On the hillside above, a column of smoke issued from beneath a prominent limestone pinnacle but there was no other sign of life. We assumed that it marked the resting place of the party we had met earlier in the day. A stream nearby provided a plentiful supply of water and we allowed ourselves two drinks, of coffee and hot lemon squash. It had been an early stop, 1.30 p.m., but a significant stage of the march seemed to have been covered. We had time to cook properly, instead of rushing against the advent of darkness, and we prepared the last of our corn and *taro* as well as *mbi* roasted *and* boiled.

The Danis were able to relax and make themselves at ease in the most uncongenial surroundings. It made an interesting comparison to watch them chatting in a comfortable group around the fire while the *tuans* sat cross-legged and awkward in wet boots and parkas under the sagging fly. When we adjourned to the *kanangda* to eat we took up more room than eleven carriers and made up a clumsy conglomeration of damp clothing, billies, eating utensils, kit-bags and boots which threatened to crowd out the fire and upset the precious cooker. Behind my back I discovered some drawings on the wall, small childish sketches in charcoal of men with bows and arrows. This was the only mark we ever discovered of any artistic inclination by the Danis. It provoked a discussion on their culture and origin.

It was not known where the tribes of New Guinea came from and our puny efforts at solving the mystery did not brighten the scene of knowledge appreciably. Duncan told of an intricately carved idol he had seen, found in the upper reaches of the Sepik River in Australian New Guinea, that had no relationship to the existing peoples; and felt that this supported a current theory that tribes such as the Dani were not of the original races inhabiting the island. Even to laymen such as ourselves it was patently obvious that the Danis, for example, had no connection with the Australian aborigine or with the Asian races in islands a comparatively short distance away, such as Bali or Borneo. They could not be easily classified under the general term of Polynesian either; the features of some might bear out the term, but those of others were radically different. The Old Codger, for instance, had a particularly Semitic appearance. Another piece of the puzzle was the tremendous diversity of language, which cannot be explained completely by the physical barriers of jungle and mountain. We were lucky in that our travels took us through the Dani area alone. A few miles to the west, at the end of the plateau, lived the Moni people with an entirely different language. At Tiom we learned to say 'Koana', but when we returned to Wamena, twenty minutes' flying time away, the word meant nothing—though the people were still known as Danis!

We began the day of 22nd June in welcome sunlight. The uncommonly warm morning allowed us to stand about in shirt-sleeves and peruse the aerial survey maps, which we spread over some tussock. We found that we were now 'on the map' and from that camp could make attempts at tracing our route. Pinpointing our camp above the Zenggilorong we followed our prospective line of travel and estimated that approximately two days would see us close to the Carstensz Noordwand. Immediately before it the map showed a very broken area. Our appetites were whetted at the thought of completely unexplored country. With any luck we might see the Noordwand that morning.

The carriers' headman came to us and asked in what direction we wished to go. It was divined that a route could be taken south-westwards towards the source of the nearby stream, or one due south past the pinnacle on the hill. The south-west route was more direct but apparently more difficult while the one to the south promised easier, if more circuitous, travelling. We chose the southern route and hastened to get away.

We moved quickly and soon passed the pinnacle on a track

Dani chiefs and tribesmen eating sweet potato (*P. Temple*)

Dani women and children—the pit has leaves for holding cooked potato
(*P. Temple*)

From the Basins of Ijomba across Lake Larson to the eastern Carstensz Range (*P. Temple*)

that wound among stunted bushes. The forest was fast disappearing behind, with no regrets on our part. An hour later we took a
last look at the hills to the north and the Zenggilorong gleaming
through crowded trees 2,000 feet below. Before us to the south
lay a deep hollow filled with a variety of ferns and tussock and
dominated by a rounded hill covered with outcrops of limestone.
To its right stood a similar hill and between the two a gently
curved saddle, which we aimed to reach. We dropped into the
hollow and Duncan was soon happily chipping away as more and
more bare rock was encountered. We wound our way through
the tree ferns and tramped hard up the southern slope towards the
saddle. Instinctively we knew what lay on the crest.

Near the top I paused to take a photograph looking back, while
Puttoh and Duncan pressed on. 'Yahoooooo! Yaaaaahoo!' As I
stuffed the camera back into my shirt Duncan's shouts echoed
among the hills. Tripping and stumbling, I scrambled breath-
lessly up the track, crashing through the ferns. And there,
beyond Puttoh's pointing ice-axe, lay the Noordwand rising
sheer into the clouds with a sliver of ice riding its flank.

H

8

The Plateau of Mists

What do the peaks prepare
For a usurper camping
Where they hold the air
And the river-bend no friend?

The plateau was at last spread out before us. The high, open country which we had begun to believe a myth, undulated out of view to the east and west, and southwards abutted against the massive limestone spine of the island. Tantalizing as ever, the clouds were rapidly settling over the mountains and within a quarter of an hour of our arrival the Noordwand was lost to view. What we had seen before the veil was drawn was almost enough to justify the months of preparation and the hard, demanding days of the trek from Tiom. We had found the Noordwand, seen the object of our dreams filling the horizon. A tongue of ice falling over its edge promised a way to the top. Beside myself with excitement, I jumped and shouted to the others to come and see.

Our saddle warranted a name: with the date as 22nd June and the shortest day of the year in the southern hemisphere, we christened it Solstice Pass. After recovering from our initial excitement we erected a cairn near by and took stock of the situation. Although the Carstensz were now less than twenty miles away the plateau was not flat by any stretch of the imagination. Our height was about 10,500 feet and rows of hills rising a thousand feet higher lay in a rolling jumble between us and the main range. The track had virtually petered out and from that point we would be dependent on the Danis' knowledge of the

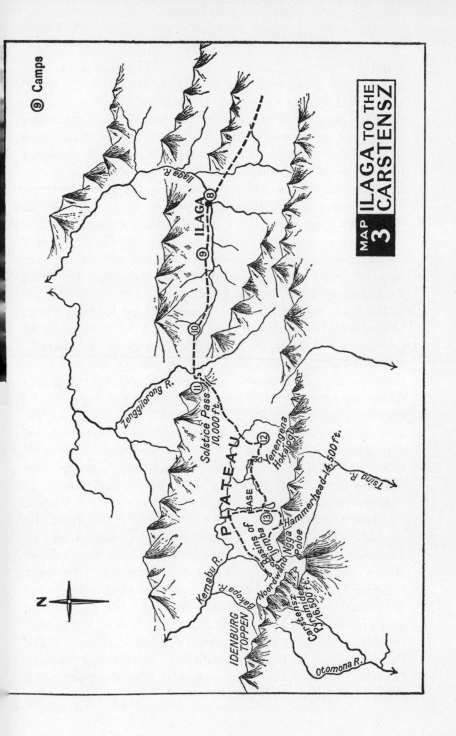

MAP **3** **ILAGA** TO THE **CARSTENSZ**

⑨ Camps

N

Ilaga R.

ILAGA ⑧

⑨

⑩

Zenggilorong R.

Solstice Pass 10,000 ft.

⑪

P-L-A-T-E-A-U

⑫

Yenengena Hoks.

Tsing R.

Hammerhead 14,500 ft.

BASE

⑬

Basins of Jojomba

Noordwand Ngga Poloe

Kemabu R.

Bakopa R.

IDENBURG TOPPEN

Carstensz Pyr. 16,500 ft.

Carstenszmidden

Otomona R.

country to guide us through the complex. The plateau was high, but not dry as we had secretly hoped. The thick clumps of tussock had a soggy footing and in the sheltered folds of the hills there was thick bush with stunted but mossy trees. Everywhere outcrops of grey, karst-weathered limestone pushed through the hillsides, giving them a battlemented aspect or the appearance of tombstones in abandoned graveyards. Karst weathering was caused by the wind and rain wearing away the softer limestone, leaving hard, resistant spikes and blocks to litter the landscape. The pastel green and yellow of the plateau rolling open and unhindered, the sight of the mountains and the knowledge that the dank, oppressive atmosphere of the forest was behind, gave us a feeling of freedom and enterprise as we dropped down into the first basin of the Kemabu River.

The basin did not possess a tributary of the Kemabu which, judging by our experiences later, received much of its water by underground drainage, but had a shallow, swampy bottom with scattered pools. These basins were as much a feature of the plateau as the hills between which they lay, and were all part of the Kemabu system which drained to the west and eventually the Pacific Ocean in Geelvink Bay. It was not long before we discovered that we were near the source of the Kemabu and that only a few miles to the east lay the sources of three other great rivers, all flowing in entirely different directions! It was apparent when we crossed the next row of hills that the beginning of an unnamed river lay within view to the south-east. This flowed due east before breaking through the main divide and eventually reached the south coast after joining with the Tjemara River; the Zenggilorong we knew rose on the plateau within a stone's throw of this and flowed due north as a main tributary of the giant Rouffaer. It was agreed that the eastwards-flowing Baliem could not rise far from our position, and then there was the Kemabu which ran due west. It was a fascinating phenomenon and another mystery of the island that warrants a detailed investigation. The Dutch New Guinea highlands, with their underground drainage, limestone caverns, lakes and rivers flowing in opposite directions, present a hydrographer's paradise.

But we did not think much of the efficiency of the drainage as we squelched through the saturated tussock and button grass. Admittedly the travelling was much easier than ever before— there were no roots to trip over—but there was no getting away from the thin, watery substance of the soil. Our hopes for better weather on the plateau had some justification early that morning, when clear skies widened over the forest mists and the sun warmed the tussock yellow across the plateau. Later in the morning clouds swept up again from both north and south, not in billowing masses of cumulus, but high and wind-harried until they breasted together over the centre of the plateau and unleashed an afternoon of rain.

We descended a short way through scattered rocks, excellent in their hidden crevices for the breakage of ankles. Beyond the basin we climbed a steep hillside to join the carriers, who had lit a fire and were placidly waiting. Tim and Dave were not in sight by this stage, having stayed behind to investigate a cave, so we delayed until they appeared before pressing on. The Danis were insistent that no one be left guideless while crossing this feature-less country, and accordingly left the Old Codger beside a signal fire to bring them on. We continued over the flat tops of the hills. A well-preserved skull lying in our path gave a grim warning to anyone foolish enough to venture on the plateau without adequate food supplies and knowledge of shelter. Coming to a faint cross-road of tracks, the headman indicated that a smear of mud running eastward was an alternative track to Ilaga. We guessed that this ran along the ridge on the eastern side of the valley, the one we had crossed from the Baliem; it proved almost con-clusively that direct access to the plateau was possible from the Baliem headwaters. We left a signpost of twigs and leaves to mark this point in case we decided to return to the mission by the new route. Duncan chipped away at rocks along the way with mount-ing excitement, since increasingly he came across signs of volcanic intrusions. This was a discovery of the first order since all the geological maps in Hollandia had vaguely shown the whole area of plateau and mountains to be limestone.

We soon began to regret leaving the shotgun at Ilaga. As was

to happen many times during the following days, Puttoh surprised a beautiful, fat quail which flapped noisily and slowly into
the air, offering a perfect target and a wholesome meal. We saw
many quail and the lakes were liberally dotted with ducks, much
to our chagrin. The Danis, although they made no attempt at
snaring or shooting birds, were quick to seize the chance of the
quail's sudden flight by plundering the eggs from the nest.

Topped with cloud, the main range nevertheless became more
and more prominent as we walked southwards. Immediately
before us, to the east of the Carstensz, the range did not rise to
any more than 14,000 feet, and long stretches were formed of
horizontal bands of limestone culminating in a perfectly flat
summit. The mountains seemed to have been thrust in one block
through the comparatively flat landscape, coloured in varying
shades of white and grey, and yet we knew that the sheer cliffs
and smooth slabs had been carved by ancient glaciers.

We stopped for lunch at the top of the southern slope of a
hill, overlooking the wide, main basin of the Kemabu. For
shelter against the threatening rain we sat under a solitary tree
strangled by moss and pressure-cooked the abominable *mbi*. Rain
it did, as we sat chewing potato and contemplating the narrow
meanders and lakelets of the river below. The temperature
dropped to remind us of our height—11,000 feet—and we were
not reluctant to don parkas and packs and move on. We waited
until Tim and Dave arrived, but as the first figure approached in
a black oilskin parka it had little resemblance to either Tim or
Dave, unless one had fallen on his face in the mud and blackened
it. It turned out to be the Old Codger, securely buttoned up in
Tim's parka; not far behind came Tim himself, holding a
pandanus raincoat over his tartan shirt. The Old Codger had been
successful at last. His whines and wheedlings had been persistent
ever since we left Ilaga; now he had presented a piteous enough
appearance and sufficient eloquent pleading to talk Tim out of
his parka. I looked at the Old Codger out of the corner of my
eye; he made a meek picture of innocent helplessness. While Tim
told us the story he hunched and cowered against the rain and
cool breeze, which his act rendered as only just within the limits

of human endurance. I almost laughed out loud at the supreme
cunning of the man. Then we turned to follow the rest of the
carriers, who were by now well across the river and trotting,
naked and unconcerned, towards the next hill.

While Tim and Dave paused for lunch we tramped down the
gentle slope to cross the river. It had nothing in common with
either the Baliem or the Zenggilorong but reminded us of the
curves and meanders of the Idenburg as seen from the air. It was
all there in miniature, a deep stream no more than fifteen feet
wide twisting sharply back and forth with side pools like ox-bow
lakes. It was deep with a strong surge rather than current and its
icy water welled up beneath our parkas as we floundered and
floated across its muddy, unstable bed. We stamped hard up the
next hill to warm our saturated legs. I cursed at wetting my feet
after carefully drying my socks the night before and assiduously
avoiding pools all morning. On the brow of the hill another guide
had been posted beside a smoky fire, since beyond him lay more
perplexing, heavily vegetated country. The next basin was much
higher than the Kemabu main stream, but not much lower than
the hill we had crossed to reach it. Beyond, a high, steep ridge
prevented a view of the range. We clambered up this, beginning
to feel the effects of a long day, and after peeping over the top at
another basin a thousand feet below, sat down with the Danis,
who were having afternoon *mbi*.

It was time to look for a camp. From the narrow ridge top we
could see on the other side of the next basin a large limestone
overhang and cave. The Danis were obviously heading for this
as there was no sign of a *kanangda* and it offered the only shelter
within view. Both features were part of the first cliff line of the
main range. The southern and eastern sides of the basin were
securely hemmed in by the slabs and blocks which towered up
4,000 feet higher into the mist. There was no grand finale to the
day's trek such as a view of the Carstensz. In their direction lay
the inevitable mist, smothering more hills and basins, dull and
uninteresting in the grey, rain-filtered light. This last basin also
had a stream, a feeder of the Kemabu. The descent was steep and
at times we had to resort to kicking steps in the soggy turf and

moss to prevent an uncontrolled slide down to the jagged karst at the bottom. We were able to cross the stream without wading, since clods of earth topped by tussock still stood firmly in the centre of the water, unaffected by the gentle surge.

We found a flat camp site on the hillside below the cave and thrashed down some high tussock to form a comfortable bed. The rain held off in the early evening but even so the Old Codger would not relinquish Tim's parka. It was a struggle to retrieve it next morning, by which time its proofing had been much diminished by the Dani's having spent the night too close to the fire.

From my diary for 23rd June:

'The country we travelled through was to be similar for most of the day—tussock and moss underfoot, sometimes wet when we approached streams or the bottoms of small valleys, sometimes dry when we approached bedrock near the hilltops. Trees grew only in small clumps bent by the rain and the weight of moss—dead tree-ferns littered the ground everywhere. Around the lakes we passed the vegetation was naturally thicker. Karst-weathered limestone lay in our path everywhere and often we would be jumping from one rock to another, careful not to slip and slide into the mossy gaps or bark a shin on the needle-like tops.'

We left Camp Twelve at 8 a.m. on the last day with carriers. There were signs that the Danis did not want to stay on the plateau any longer than was absolutely necessary. This was entirely understandable, since that first night spent in the mountains, at almost 11,000 feet, was as cold as Camp Seven on the tops before we reached Ilaga. Their exposed rock bivouac did not radiate comfort and it was some time before they had worked enough warmth into their limbs to start out.

We dropped down on to the stream's southern bank and after walking due west for a few hundred yards entered a shallow, rock-filled valley which took us a little deeper into the mountains. It was not long before we swerved westward again, climbed to a saddle between two low hills and looked down on an extensive lake. 'Hey, look at that!' shouted Duncan. The lake had held our attention, but on following Duncan's pointing finger we looked up and saw a great vertical wall topped with ice, almost imperceptible against the background of grey cloud. It was only a few miles distant. We were nearly there.

It was apparent as we dropped down through a small wood of tree-ferns that the headman was not now sure of his ground. Throughout the day his progress was marked by frequent consultations with his companions. He had shown some hesitation when approaching the saddle and when, a short distance later, we passed a well-kept *kanangda* it was clear that these Danis had no previous knowledge of its existence, otherwise they would surely have chosen the site to camp. It was only half an hour's travel from the overhang camp and showed that we were still close to the trading route to the southern jungle villages. Below the *kanangda* the lake stretched from north to south, securely held in its southern reaches by high cliffs, which leaned in great overhangs over the water. At one point a sizable waterfall gushed from the cliff face with no discernible stream or spring to feed it. We were forced northward, following the lake's eastern verge and at times wading through the shallow and crystal-clear water on white, rocky beaches. There was no sign of fish though Dave picked up some tiny shells. Ducks were dotted out beyond our reach.

We had pinpointed our position on the map but its vagueness meant that we were not without the feeling of continuing discovery as each new feature of the virgin country appeared before us. At its northern end the lake emptied in a wide, shallow stream to a second lake lying east to west. Through painstaking inquiries Duncan learned from the Danis that the lakes were known as Yenengena Hokajogu. As we climbed the hill of the peninsula between the two, our old plan of a seaplane landing in the mountains came flooding back. The second lake was ideal for such a venture, long and narrow with no obstruction and a rise in the land at the western end of no more than fifteen or twenty feet. Puttoh's plans to build an airship to float around this windless country were temporarily eclipsed by visions of a huge base camp beside the water, regularly replenished from the air with mountains of supplies—tents, air mattresses, duckboards, fruit, tables, stoves, cake, kettles, steak and in particular tea, which was now just a treasured memory.

The idea was not so fanciful since the mammoth 1938–9 expedition, led by the American millionaire Archbold, had only been possible with aerial supply from a twin-engined Catalina amphibian. From 'The Guba', as it was called, Archbold had first discovered the Grand Baliem valley and subsequently made regular landings on Habbema Lake and on the Wamena River (close by the present Government post) to supply the scores of men he had employed in scientific research. He ascertained whether the lake was deep enough for a landing by the simple expedient of flying low over the water, dangling a weighted line. We felt inclined to make soundings to save future expeditions from the long trek, but the icy water and lack of time pushed us on.

Turning south-westward we arrived at the summit of a prominent hill and looked towards the mountains once more. They had disappeared into the lowering mantle of cloud and but for our faith and limited knowledge of their existence there was nothing to reassure us that they lay anywhere within the next fifty miles. Before us were two more basins divided by a low hill and a torrential stream bounding over a bouldery bed, at variance to the streams we had so far encountered on the plateau. But then, nothing was surprising in this complex of weird watersheds. The ground was becoming more rocky and there were bare patches of pulverized limestone alternating with the karst. We seemed to have reached an impasse. The way was barred by more cliffs and steep ridges. To the west a high whaleback ridge dominated the view. Its lower reaches seemed to offer the only means of further progress.

We followed the carriers across the first basin, climbed the hill beyond the stream and descended to the second basin bisected by a further stream, silent and deep like the Kemabu. We paused for lunch and consulted our maps once more. They showed little of the high, broken hills surrounding us. The headman took a close but puzzled interest as Duncan brought his sketch-maps and notebook up to date. Eager to solve the mystery of our route we walked on as soon as possible. We were at the base of cliffs and heading towards the steepest part of the whaleback, which had us completely confounded. With little warning a side valley opened out to the south, burying itself among the precipices of the surrounding heights. Its eastern flank was sheer, a white limestone face that would offer a knotty problem to the best of the Dolomite experts. The top of the face was overhung and we wasted little time walking beneath it, hopping over chunks of rock which had obviously fallen recently. The western flank was no more encouraging, its little walls and steep slopes covered in tangled scrub. The southern end was similar, prompting us to name the valley the Cul-de-sac. Our headman seemed as baffled as we were, though a handful of carriers had pushed on confidently, indicating that there must be a route offering escape.

It was difficult to trace the faint track amongst the tussock and it took some careful searching before we were able to follow it to the south-eastern corner of the valley. It ended against rock and gnarled bushes. The vanguard of carriers had disappeared. We followed the faint traces of their movement, twisted grass and disturbed earth, and after climbing an awkward rock wall entered a steep gully arched with trees. It was very steep and full of stinging nettles, which did not improve our temper as we groaned and laboured upward. This gully, was the key, however, for as we emerged from its head and walked across the ridge, the lower slopes of the main divide came into view once more.

A shallow, rocky gully descended the southern slopes of the ridge and the two provided a perfect corridor through the barrier of cliffs. I stopped to take a photograph looking down into the Cul-de-sac and then, on joining Lynn, looked astounded past his raised camera at a huge tower. Its vertical sides rose straight as a ruler into the infuriating clouds, which allowed us only a brief glimpse before they swirled lazily to cloak its magnificence.

To catch the others we ran down the Corridor. It widened to give yet another surprise. Another lake unfolded and another whaleback to the south-west. Beyond both, sharp, contorted rock peaks leaned to the south with smooth, twisted slabs at their feet. Duncan was talking to the carriers when we arrived at a point overlooking the lake; it transpired that they intended to leave us the next morning. They had brought us to the *dugundugoo*—the rest was up to us.

With this news in mind, Puttoh formulated a plan. The airdrop was due on Tuesday, 27th June, and we had three clear days before then. The question arose: Should we merely use those days for setting up Base Camp and preparing for the drop, or should we begin a reconnaissance of the range immediately? Puttoh did not mince matters. 'We can't afford to waste time. If the airdrop fails, and we've just twiddled our thumbs waiting for it, we'll be going home empty handed. There isn't enough food to stay beyond Wednesday. On the other hand, if we put in a couple of three-day recces and the airdrop's a muck-up we might at least solve the problem of access to and up the Noordwand. Duncan and I will shoot up on the whaleback tonight in the hope of catching a good view of the Carstensz in the morning. We might be able to give the rest of you some clues on the country, and possible recce routes to take. Also we've got to find a good spot to receive the drop. The whaleback, if it's broad enough, might be just the answer. If we want you to join us in the morning we'll light a fire before 7 a.m. and you'll have to persuade the Danis to carry up. Otherwise wait for us to come back.'

We angled down through steep scrub to the western end of the lake, crossed its outlet and set up Camp Thirteen a hundred yards from the water's edge. The weather so far today had been perfect, a flood of sunlight. The sky was still comparatively clear with no threat of rain. Could our weather luck have changed at last? There was no view to the west and north from the camp since we were lodged close beneath the steep slopes of the whale-back. The lake stretched for about a mile to the east, ending in cliffs and hills, but a suggestion of low saddles confirmed the Danis' statement that a pass lay across them, leading beyond the mountains to the south. Our bank provided the only flat border of the lake. We were situated amongst scattered trees, which petered out to the south against a prominent spur which formed the southern cliff-line above the water. Our only chance of advancing beyond the lake to the south lay in two indentations on this spur. Their approaches did not entail cliff climbing or bushwhacking, though to reach the second, which lay at the very eastern end of the spur, would mean an awkward traverse around the scrub-smothered edges of the lake.

We had the fire going immediately and cooked some *mbi* for an early tea so that Puttoh and Duncan would not be bothered with firelighting in their high bivouac. They gulped down the mash, pocketed two roast potatoes each for breakfast, and set off without more ado, taking the fly for shelter.

The airdrop, the crux of our journey, was rapidly approaching, and I could not help thinking that despite our success so far the only hope of continued advance was focused on one brief half-hour on Tuesday morning. I was filled with anxiety and held no confidence in the success of the drop. If Steiger had been coming, flying low, manœuvring through the valleys in his light plane, I could have confidently looked forward to peaches and cream for Tuesday dinner. But the thought of a lumbering Dakota turning slowly in the clouds above the hills brought back the floury taste of *mbi*.

With an early dinner under our belts we could relax in daylight for a change. Grasping the opportunity with both hands we spread out our damp clothes to dry in the last precious hours of sunlight. I lay back in my down jacket under a tree and savoured the view of the lake, eyeing a bevy of fat ducks floating complacently near the bank. One of the Danis had a bow but no amount of persuasion would make him risk an arrow across the water. I wandered down to the bank and disconsolately tossed pebbles as the smug birds quietly paddled out of reach.

Quickly the sky greyed. As I walked back to the tent a shower of hail came sweeping across the lake. There was a short period of chaos as we lunged around the fire hastily snatching clothes, then we dived into the tent with arms full as the hail whipped through the camp. 'Blast the b—— weather!' someone shouted as we crouched under the tent flap. That sentiment summed up our general opinion of the wicked clouds, which could not desist from niggling at our patience. I looked around my companions but could not discover even the faintest resemblance to a tan. The amount of sun we had received during the journey would make London seem like Aden in comparison. It was noticeable that as the trek progressed we drank less and less until our evening cup of coffee became only a habit, appreciated more for its warmth than its liquid content. I became a firm believer in the theory that enough moisture can be absorbed through the skin to satisfy a fit body's demands. Disgusted, I threw my saturated trousers into the murk. Our thoughts went out to Puttoh and Duncan, the two who would be receiving the brunt of the storm.

There was no *kanangda* near the camp site and the Danis had been forced to throw up a temporary shelter, a flimsy structure of twisted branches and tussock. It was a porous affair and they resorted largely to a small fire and their pandanus coats to ward off the hail and rain. Just after nightfall we were allowed a limited view of the moon between the faint lines of scudding clouds. Mists swarmed up the face of a milky-white cliff to the east. It grew cold. As frost set in I was thankful for the warmth of my '20 Below' sleeping-bag. It was the first frost we had experienced and it woke me several times during the night. Half asleep, I heard the Danis chanting in a doleful attempt to ward off the biting night air.

We were reluctant to leave our bags the following morning. No long march was immediately in prospect, frigid air pervaded the grey light of dawn and there were no shouts of 'Nawok!' from Puttoh and Duncan. When we did finally crawl out of the tent, in time to watch for the fire at 7 a.m., the Danis still cowered in their shelter, silent and subdued. The only sign of their presence lay in the thin spiral of smoke rising through their sagging roof. I walked down to the edge of the lake to obtain a wide view of the ridge and waited for the fire signal. Seven o'clock came and went without sign and after a while I walked back to the tent with the news that Puttoh and Duncan were probably on their way down.

By this time the Danis had crept from their shelter and stood shivering and huddled together, plainly voicing their intention to go home. Filled with wonder at their hardihood and ability to stand up to the demoralizing climate, I could not blame them. We could not let them go immediately, however, since there might have been a change of plan resulting from Puttoh's reconnaissance. It was Duncan's prerogative also to make out the note to be taken back to Larson authorizing the payment of axes. We could only assuage their protestations with '*Tuan* Duncan, *awo imay*', pointing up to the whaleback. They trotted back and forth to the shelter, hiding from the cold. But the Old Codger lingered by the fire with characteristic whines and fingered my down jacket, in the manner of a shrewd merchant after a good bargain.

We delayed breakfast for Puttoh and Duncan. Eventually, at half past nine, we heard their shouts through the trees. They appeared looking a little the worse for wear but obviously full of news. As soon as he reached the fire, and without removing his pack, Puttoh launched into a description of their movements.

After leaving camp they had travelled to the south for half a mile, leaving the lakeside, and had struck directly up towards the summit of the whaleback. The slope had been reasonable lower down but at the time of the hailstorm they were faced with a cliff wall of sticky and half-frozen conglomerate. Lashed by the storm, they had been forced to cut steps in the cliff. It was with some relief that they finally reached the stunted bushes on its crest at about 11,500 feet. To their disappointment the whaleback was not as wide as they had hoped and had soon proved useless as an air-drop site. A sheer, thousand-foot face was discovered on the other side. When they reached the top, a limited view was obtained of the Noordwand lying just a few miles away beyond a complex of ridges and peaks.

The night was one that they would surely care to forget; it had been considerably colder than in our sheltered position and the fly had offered little protection. When they woke in the morning a film of ice covered the plastic, up to an inch thick in the folds. There was virtually no view at first light and they set off along the crest of the ridge, trying to locate a site for base camp and airdrop. 'We found the ideal spot', Puttoh said, 'about a couple of miles down the valley from the lake. It's wide and open with a swampy bottom—that might save the boxes from too much damage if they're dropped from a couple of hundred feet.' A suitable shelf for the tent had been discovered and then they had returned to Camp Thirteen.

Although little view had been obtained it was possible to decide

that a promising line of advance lay to the south, over the spur
and then westwards beneath the main divide. Any other move
would mean circling the whaleback and westward ridges to find
a valley penetrating the Noordwand. We finally relieved Puttoh
of his pack and handed both of them the pot of *mbi*.

The Danis had appeared *en masse* with Duncan's arrival. At
their clamourings he had quickly written out their note. Clutching the precious piece of paper they prepared to leave but not
without attempting to return to us the *jums* and pandanus
coats we had purchased for them in Ilaga. In their view these were
our property, and there was no suggestion that they could quietly
make off with them without our permission. This was granted of
course and there was a look of joy in their faces as they bid us
goodbye. We shook hands with everyone amid a confused babble
of *koanas*. Even the Old Codger seemed happy, though he kept
a sharp eye out for anything else to supplement the coat and
jum. Their chatter faded away. They ran off towards the Corridor
and were soon lost in the scrub.

Now the main reconnaissances could begin. Puttoh decided
that Lynn and I should start that day in an attempt to reach the
Noordwand. After we had gone, the rest of the party would move
down to the site chosen for Base Camp and make preparations for
the drop. The next day, Sunday, Tim and Dave would leave to
investigate the feasibility of reaching the Dajak Pass, which
Colijn's expedition had reached from the southern side in 1936.
If Lynn and I failed to find access up the Noordwand—and to our
main objective, the Pyramide—then the pass might offer a
suitable alternative and a lower packing route on to the glaciers.

Lynn and I packed up, taking the fly for shelter and the rope
for climbing. We had three days' supply of European food and the
pressure-cooker, but no primus stove as we anticipated a plentiful
supply of firewood in our bivouacs, which would be, in every case,
below the tree line. Our medical kit consisted of a couple of bandages
and a handful of terramycin pills, issued with strict instructions by
Duncan, to counter any serious illness such as pneumonia.

We had an early lunch and then, in threatening weather, set off
to the south at 11.15 a.m.

Scree slide and route up North Wall of the Carstensz Pyramide (*P. Temple*)

A point overlooking the lake near Camp 13. *See* page 109. (*L. S. Crawford*)

The Zenggilorong River. Sitting astride felt infinitely more secure than the first walk across. *See* page 148. (*D. E. Cooper*)

9

The Basins of Ijomba

The door of the valley
Swings shut behind.
But in the next gully
Who knows but I'll find
The colour to make all tongues wag.

As Lynn and I walked along the shores of the lake I became more and more conscious of the privilege we had in exploring unknown country. Now there were no Danis to guide us, no information from previous explorers; the land was ours to discover. We had a trail to blaze, a goal to achieve, which required the unravelling of the ridges and the probing of the mountain defences.

Our first objective was the valley which lay hidden behind the east–west spur. From there an attempt could be made to break out to the west along the foot of the main divide's face, or to follow a weakness in the face upwards, until a traverse along the range could be accomplished.

Of the two indentations mentioned earlier, the more eastern of the two, where the valley issued into the lake, seemed most promising. Accordingly we followed the curve of the bank intending to sidle along the water's edge beneath the spur's cliffs. However, when we came hard up against the problem, we found the way impassable from overhanging scrub, which jutted out from its tenacious grip on the precipitous slopes and forced us into the water. Rebuffed at the start, we turned to the only alternative. The second indentation lay higher on the spur before

I 115

it abutted on to the whaleback, and so we climbed steep tussock slopes alongside a tangle of scrub. Making our way through the tussock was as hard as breaking a trail in deep, new snow. The clumps of tough grass had to be stamped down and the pitfalls of hidden streams and holes avoided like crevasses and snow-covered rocks. It became soggier as the slope steepened, and as we approached the indentation we took the precaution of kicking steps. Thankfully no cliff wall barred our way and a few minutes later we stood on its crest and faced a wall of vegetation. It looked like being a long day thrashing through trees.

Without a bush knife we sought the line of least resistance, rather than attempt progress in any particular direction. After breaking a few branches out of our path, we found a comparatively easy passage, ducking and twisting down the mossy hillside. We removed as much of the vegetation's barrier as possible and assiduously blazed and snapped twigs as we went.

We emerged into a dry, glacial basin at about the same height as the lake and filled with karst. Below a jagged line of rocks lay a second basin and this opened out into the unwatered valley. We could not see the summit of the mountains for cloud, but it was immediately apparent that no way lay farther south up the uninviting cliffs and waterfalls. The rain arrived as we tramped on to the western end of the valley, eager to discover a key to further progress. It was almost as if our visit had been anticipated. Between the high, vertical edges of the whaleback and the main face lay a gently curved saddle; it even had a streak of tussock dividing the scrub to its crest. We ascended directly and shortly looked on to a new view. A long, open gully fell at our feet to a circular, swampy valley head. On the other side a ridge swept up to 12,000 feet. Above our level towards its south end lay another saddle, just beneath the cloud base. 'Might as well head for that,' remarked Lynn. I agreed and plunged down the gully after him. At the bottom we picked our way carefully across the swamp and as we did so a valley opened out to the north, and the cliff which Puttoh and Duncan had discovered the previous evening came into view. A stream rushed from a gorge-like valley and we followed this, up towards the second saddle. It was unpleasant work pushing through dripping bushes, while the rain swirled in curtains of mist. We crossed the stream several times, hopping from one slimy boulder to another, until we entered an enclosed basin at its head. At times we came across trampled tussock, almost forming tracks, but we dismissed them as made by ant-eaters, which were reputed to inhabit the plateau—until we discovered the remains of fires. It then seemed likely that Dani hunters penetrated the upper basins, seeking the warm ant-eater skin. We were puzzled, however, by the way the charred sticks radiated like the spokes of a wheel. This was not a common Dani method of fire construction.

The stream was fed by an impressive waterfall which cascaded over the line of cliffs. Cliffs seemed to be an inevitable feature of our southern flank, effectively barring any attempt at penetration to the peaks above. Duncan had described this waterfall as a prominent feature of their view and had mentioned a shelf above it which might simplify a climb up the face. From our position below, the shelf was clearly evident but there was no obvious way to reach it. Nor was it clear that it would offer any solution to the whereabouts of the Noordwand. We estimated that we had travelled three or four miles to the west since leaving camp. According to our calculation we must be very close to the wall's eastern limit. But the puzzle remained—were the cliffs and shelf the beginnings of the Noordwand, or did it lie farther to the west, or did the range above lie before it? The increasing intensity of the rain and the persistent cloud put an end to further speculation.

We crouched beneath a tree and lunched. This time it was scroggin and chocolate instead of *mbi*. We carefully chewed every scrap, savouring the familiar taste after a week's denial. I smoked a cigarette and counted the contents of my last tin. I had just enough cigarettes to see me through to the airdrop. By Tuesday lunch time at the latest they would run out. But by then I expected to be rifling the store I had spread through three containers for safety.

After some discussion we agreed to climb to the saddle and there decide on our next move. It was a long pull to the top and I was breathless not only from the exertion but also from excitement at the prospect of a revealing view from the top. We were disappointed. As we tramped over the final rise we were met by an icy wind—and no view save that of a grassy, rectangular basin a few feet below, ending in boulders and a background of shrouded rock. The climb to the saddle had given us some advantage, however, since we were now no more than 100 feet below the edge of the cliffs on our left. To our right the 12,000-foot ridge was a similar height above, presenting a vertical edge.

It was three o'clock. We saw little point in continuing blindly into the rain and mist without first establishing with some accuracy our position in relation to the Noordwand. We might have easily bypassed a significant route to its foot. More than that, the slabs which we could now see vaguely in the clouds had definitely been subject to glaciation and the possibility of striking an icecap a few hundred feet higher could not be lightly dismissed. The Noordwand, steep and perhaps vertical, had to be found, and also routes to its crest, for there lay the glaciers and the Pyramide. We resolved to camp, but certainly not in the basin before us— it had no water and provided an excellent funnel for the bitter wind, which grew more powerful each minute.

A slide of boulders offered a convenient, if awkward, staircase to the shelf, and we pulled ourselves up it, leaving the wind behind. The shelf held the final line of low trees and scrub which petered out on its upper edge. Although criss-crossed with hollows and fissures, its main feature was the several huge rocks, suspiciously like erratics, left behind by an ancient glacier or, at this point, an icefall. Duncan would have rejoiced at the variety of rock features we encountered over the next two days.

We chose a hollow for the bivouac, sheltered on one side by a bunch of trees and on the other by one of the great boulders. We erected the fly at a low angle to escape the powerful gusts of wind that eddied along the shelf. A length of nylon cord was employed to support the sheet of plastic, which we draped over it like a blanket over a clothes-line. The ends of the cord were secured to a tree and the great boulder respectively, while the four corners of the fly were pulled out and tied to ice-axes and branches. Although there was plenty of length in the fly, twelve feet, its width was a little too narrow to be completely comfortable. Of the eight feet, two were lost in providing the angle of the roof. Nevertheless, we knew that the material was absolutely impervious. We could be guaranteed a dry night's rest provided the wind did not blow the rain at an angle.

While Lynn prepared the dried vegetables for soaking in the pressure-cooker, I knelt to the absorbing task of lighting a fire. To aid me I had Puttoh's heavy sheath-knife for chipping kindling, a box of matches and a candle. As every boy scout knows, these are ample tools for lighting a fire. Before leaving, Dave had illustrated to us the Dani trick of obtaining crisp, dry tussock from the sheltered roots of trees. We had wisely taken the precaution of stowing some in our packs when we set out. The rain held off as I eagerly chipped flakes of wood on top of the tussock, visualizing the hot stew that would be ours in half an hour's time. 'We'll wait until the embers are really red hot before we put the pot on,' I remarked to Lynn. 'Good-oh!' I applied a match, sheltering it from the faint breeze. The tussock flared and shrivelled up without making the feeblest attempt at igniting the chips. Too many chips, I thought, and carefully arranged the kindling for a second attempt.

The damp ground was littered with match-sticks. Lynn and I stared grimly at the pile of slightly charred wood which was the result of over an hour's continuous effort. I cursed quietly as both of us shivered violently in damp clothes. I put on my down jacket, slipped into my sleeping-bag and reapplied myself. Lynn huffed himself blue in the face, we burnt half a candle, even crawled out of the warmth of our bags to find new wood, but nothing would induce the miserable twigs to burn. I was furious. Then I began to laugh at the ridiculous situation, at our lack of foresight in not carrying the primus. None of us had raised a finger to light fires until that day. It had always been left to the Danis—and we had let them go without gathering their secrets—the wood to choose, the way to apply it, the way to light it. On top of that we were at 12,000 feet, where the oxygen content of the atmosphere would be markedly less than in the moss forest, and the vegetation was dripping with water.

Darkness was approaching, so we abandoned the idea of a hot meal until next day and made do with a cold supper. Although it was a curious mixture—nutmeat, biscuits, butter, honey, marmite, raspberry drink and acid drops—our palates were tickled by the unaccustomed variety of flavours. We suddenly appreciated the real value of butter, which we had taken for granted in New Zealand, and ate it by the chunk with spoonfuls of marmite.

The bivouac was very snug. We could afford to smile as the rain pattered ineffectually on the plastic and we lay warmly cocooned in our bags and covers. Our meandering talk drifted with my cigarette smoke into the evening. Incidents in the Baliem were recalled, the inevitable discussion arose on the forthcoming airdrop and plans for the next day were mooted. The wind roared across the rocks above and occasionally sneaked a blow at us, raising the edge of the fly with a noisy flap.

Daylight brought no respite from the low cloud and rain. The storm still rushed over us and we began to see the precious hours of our reconnaissance frittered away by the weather. We made a half-hearted decision to make a move by midday. If the weather improved we would climb up the face but if not we would descend to the next valley in the hope of finding more willing firewood. We dozed the morning away with frequent glances skywards. Imperceptibly the rock towers above came into view, the wind began to arrive in gusts rather than long sweeps and the interval between each grew longer and longer. Skiffs of snow lay along the ledges only a few hundred feet higher.

At 11.30 a.m. we stirred decisively, anxious to get into action. We had a quick lunch of scroggin and sweets and then crawled stiffly into the open to feel the damp coldness briskly vaporize our clinging warmth. We left the removal of our down jackets until last, after we had carefully stowed our gear beneath the fly, and packed one mule with spare clothing and the rope. The rain had abated by the time we set off and we made for a low limestone wall. This was a little to the west and lay between two high towers. It proved to be an awkward obstacle and we only surmounted it by dint of much pulling and pushing through cascades of hardy scrub and up steps of sharp rock. Above the wall lay a

short, easy scree slope finishing at a line of slabs. We took to these
with vigour, refreshed at the feel of clean, firm rock beneath our
hands. But we made an awkward job of it at first as we tried to
readjust our limbs to an easy climbing rhythm after the uneven
gait required by the forest and plateau. Almost immediately I
lacerated a third finger by taking too energetic a grip on a spiky
rib of karst. As we began climbing, the comparative efficiency of
our footwear became apparent. Whereas Lynn's nailed boots had
been of value on the slimy logs of the forest, my rubbers came
into their own on the rock.

Our view was still badly limited by cloud and we could pick
out no prominent peak or col to fix on. Instead we zigzagged
steadily upwards, seeking the easiest line of ascent. We soon
realized as each belt of slabs was topped that no sight of ice would
reward our efforts. We were certainly not on the Noordwand and
our hopes became pinned on a possible view from the summit of
the range.

We rounded a soaring buttress and stood on a flat shelf as the
clouds parted below and revealed the plateau. The dull grey and
green rolled away to the north and we could see the lake and the
Cul-de-sac clearly. But there was no intimation of Base Camp and
its smoke. We were startled by the view to the east, where the
range was divided by a deep gap. Beyond we saw a second plateau
ending abruptly at a line of forest-clad hills. It swam slowly out of
sight as more sagging clouds advanced towards us, but not before
it added one more puzzle to our plans. We surmised, rightly as it
turned out, that the new plateau held the Tsing River, which
rose at the end of the Noordwand. The Carstensz must be only a
stone's throw away.

To continue our ascent we chose a deep and wide fault running
by the eastern flank of the buttress. Patches of snow were
encountered between the clumps of tussock, which effectively
screened deep potholes and, on one occasion, a wicked-looking
cave which defied our attempts at plumbing with stones. On our
left hand a high face of rock looked like a loosely fitted jigsaw, its
wriggling cracks and curves stuffed with stunted grass.

'We're getting nowhere fast,' I said to Lynn as we emerged

from the top of the fault and took in the view of more corrugated limestone rising to a ridge at right angles across our path. Time was pressing. It was the middle of the afternoon. If we wished to move our bivouac that day we could not afford to push on much farther. The weather seemed to be closing down again; as thick mists swallowed up the vestiges of our view we began to fear losing the route down the slabs. Before we became too down-hearted we scrambled to a spiky summit which marked the crest of the buttress behind us. This was our consolation prize, which we estimated had a height of about 14,000 feet; we named it Flying Buttress because of its obvious configuration, supporting the higher ridge. We descended and sat in a sheltered spot as it began spitting with rain.

As I finished my cigarette Lynn said: 'We might as well head back.' I was niggled by the thought that we had neither found nor seen anything important. I stood up. 'Let's just go to the top of this next ridge. We've got time and, you never know, we might see something interesting.' Lynn led the way. We crossed extensive snow patches and after negotiating a small chimney we climbed the last stretch of steep rock. 'Well, well!' said Lynn, stopping suddenly on the crest. I went up beside him and looked down a tremendous face which plummeted out of sight into the cloud. We climbed a little higher to a blocky peak and waited for the view to improve.

As the clouds began to thin we heard the steady roar of a river far below. We strained to see through the blankness until a line of buttresses began to take shape, and then a section of the southern plateau, and then the river, the Tsing itself. The face fell about 2,000 feet to a broad shelf topping the buttresses, and these in turn fell a further 2,000 feet to the river. The buttresses looked rotten—a decaying pile of stones knit together with clay.

Our position was clearer though not pinpointed. Overlooking the Tsing which, judging by its size, was near its source, we stood on the divide of a range lying east of the Carstensz. The lie of the land suggested that the Noordwand was somewhat south of west, but in that direction there were massive piles of cloud. No further light could be thrown on the situation. The sun came out in spasmodic flashes and it appeared as though the weather was breaking. We waited as long as we dared for the skies to clear but there was nothing doing. We began the descent, leaving our peak, the Hammerhead, behind. We decided that our best move would be to travel farther west the next day and attempt to cross or break through the range to strike the Noordwand at right angles. With this in mind we reached the bivouac after 4 p.m. and packed up, aiming to gain as much ground as possible that afternoon.

Our first step was to reach the western extremity of the shelf, and as we picked our way through the rocks and fissures a light shower of rain blew over our heads, creating a double rainbow arched above the bivouac site. I felt in a good mood. The weather seemed to be clearing, my limbs were pleasurably tired from climbing, and more of the delightfully intricate system of hills and basins was revealed as we descended. We turned northwards from the bar of high ridges and dropped from one basin to another seeking the next main valley. It was still and quiet after the cloud-swept slabs, warmer and more peaceful as the sun condescended to warm our backs. We jogged along and eventually reached the edge of a basin overlooking a wide valley. A bivouac site was selected below and we pushed through the bush clothing the steep descent. The slope suddenly turned to bluffs and our progress turned from a jog to a scramble, with treacherous footing. Moss and bushes still clung to the near vertical rock and with these to aid us we swung from branch to branch, our feet occasionally digging niches in the thin layer of moss. Lower down the vegetation grew thicker as the angle eased and we bullocked our way through to the open, packs covered in a collection of twigs and leaves. 'Whew!' That was enough for one day. As we made our way to the preselected bivouac we looked back at the bluff line and saw that by a sheer fluke we had desended between two lines of cliffs which must have forced a dubious rappel had we not stumbled on the one easier route.

We set up our second bivouac in a wide basin above the valley. A roaring waterfall thrashed down the bluffs of our descent. We had chosen the only comparatively dry spot in the basin, about two feet above the general level, and our feet sank rather than squelched into the turf. Nearby, a tangle of dead trees promised good fuel for a fire. Our route for the next day was obvious: to drop farther to the valley, round the end of the ridge, and penetrate southwards towards the Noordwand once more.

When I pulled the pressure-cooker from my pack I let out a groan of dismay. The stew which had been soaking in it had spilled and now clung stickily to its sides. Exploring further I pulled out my sleeping-bag, throughly laced with mixed vegetables, then tacky clothing and equipment; beyond the streak of stew a gritty puddle filled the bottom of my pack. The expletives that filled the air after this discovery seemed to stun Lynn, who squatted silent and sympathetic as I threw my possessions in fury over the bushes in a vain hope that they would dry. Illogically my annoyance turned to the problem of firemaking and I was grimly determined that we should not be a second night without a hot meal. We gathered handfuls of dry tussock from the roots of the trees and carefully selected a pile of dryish twigs.

At first we had no success. The tussock burned but the twigs would not catch fire. I began to look in despair at the cold concoction which Lynn had prepared in the cooker. Applying another match I fed the little crackling flames with more and more tussock until a large yellow mound lay smoking feebly in the dusk. But it had the required effect. When we pulled it gently apart to allow the circulation of more air, we found a hot, red core. We applied the twigs and to our great delight they began to smoke over the concentrated heat and soon we were treated to a reluctant flame. 'Eureka!' I shouted, and we appointed ourselves New Guinea Firelighters, First Class.

Even so we hardly dared breathe as the flame caressed the thick base of the cooker. There was not sufficient heat to create a high pressure and there was no hissing from the valve. After forty-five minutes we lifted the lid and found a hot, cooked stew. Before eating this we had to decide whether to use the remaining heat for a drink or for a rice pudding and we plumped for the latter, replacing the cooker as soon as the stew was removed. Half an hour later I sat back and wrote in my diary: 'Never have we had a better meal since leaving Tiom.' I was no longer discontented,

not even when I scraped the bits of stew from my bag and pulled
it over my shoulders with the aroma of stale, uncooked vegetables
hovering around my nostrils.

The evening was still and settled, the only sound coming from
the distant roar of the waterfall. The fire smoked gently at our
heads and the sky, filled with fleecy clouds, a wealth of stars and
an almost full moon, beautified our little camp.

We woke to a shivery but dry morning. Our toes quickly
froze when we pulled on our damp socks, so that we wasted no
time in moving away after a cold breakfast. We left the forlorn
fly behind and meandered across the basin until we found an easy
crossing of the wide stream. Then, trying to stamp our feet into
life, we made for the basin's edge and the valley below. Again we
were confronted by steep bluffs. Lynn, who carried the pack for
the first part of the day, had a trying time as we gingerly climbed
down, hanging to the moss and loose rock by the skin of our teeth
and at times enveloped in the spray of an adjacent waterfall. On
reaching the valley bottom we turned the ridge and began to
move southwards towards the source of the Kemabu-like river,
which flowed to the north.

Grey cloud was low once more and as usual we had no certain
knowledge of where we were going, or what really lay beyond
the head of the valley. Between the two ridges holding the head
was a line of low, bush-covered hills and beyond them a rampart
of cliffs which seemed to stretch unbroken across our path.
Beyond these, nothing save a screen of cloud. We had little choice
but to advance and examine the defences of the cliffs.

Not relishing a crossing of the river we stuck to its eastern
bank in the hope that upstream it would grow narrow enough to
let us jump across. We found a better method than that. Before
we reached the hills the river disappeared or rather appeared from
the ground, gushing strongly from an outcrop of limestone. This
simplified the problem considerably and we merely walked
around the river. We moved across the basin towards the whaleback, watching for a promising gap. We kept moving without
rest or pause.

After some meanderings and false leads we made a serious bid to cross the hills at their lowest point. Uncannily the trees opened before us and we found an easy tunnel through to the southern slopes. A glint of water caught my eye and with each step forward a lake grew bigger, filling the view. From the water's edge, all seemed of no avail. Cliffs sprang out of the lake on all sides. Then, on the far eastern side, we saw the faint colour of tussock running up to a notch at the top of the cliffs. Above towered a beautiful, curled peak, which we spontaneously called the Fang. We were not beaten yet and decided to cross the cliffs *via* the tussock route.

If we thought that we were the first to see the lake, we were mistaken, for near where we stood a long stick had been driven into the ground. Its end showed signs of having been hewn from a tree—conclusive evidence that the Danis, or some other people, had penetrated that far. The lake demanded a photograph. The sun was out and the water glittered. As Lynn wound on the film after his first shot he said quietly: 'Look at that.' There, above the southern clifftop rose a high tower, magnificent in its snowcap and the huge plume of white cloud that billowed off it. We let out bellows of joy—we had found the key.

When we reached the edge of the lake we felt that an apt name would be Lake Discovery. It was a beautiful lake, blue, enhanced by the sunlight, and made imposing by its guardian white cliffs and the serrated ridges that lunged into the sky on each hand. Water gushed from the lake in twin streams, which promptly disappeared into the ground after running their courses for no more than a few yards, and even here there were fat, complacent ducks. We walked along the edge and found the ideal site for an advance base camp (height about 11,500 feet). It was a wide, flat platform above the water and would receive the sun all day, if it shone. We could already visualize the six of us tramping across the country with heavy loads and dumping the airdrop supplies in this idyllic sanctuary.

To reach the foot of the tussock route we were obliged to cross two hillocks overlooking the lake. With future passages in mind we carefully picked the best way over them and through the bush. We frequently signposted our trail with blazes on the tree-trunks.

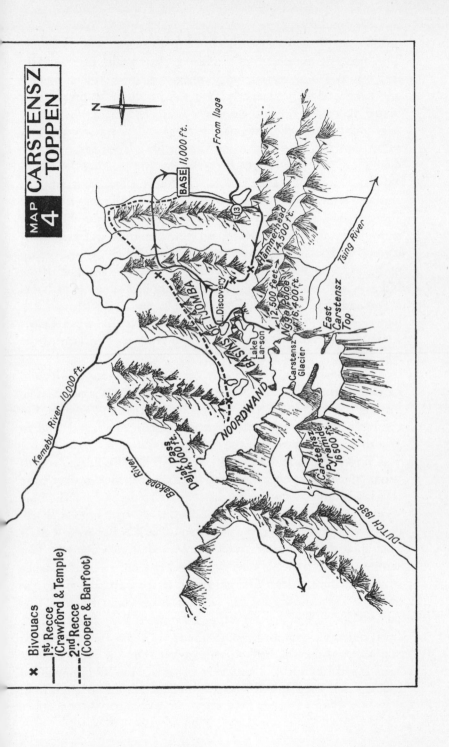

MAP 4 CARSTENSZ TOPPEN

× Bivouacs
— 1st Recce (Crawford & Temple)
--- 2nd Recce (Cooper & Barfoot)

N

Kemabu River 10,000 ft.

Bakopa River

Dajak Pass 11,000 ft.

NOORDWAND

Tomba

BATHS

Discovery

Lake Larson

12,500 feet

Ngga Pulu 16,400 ft.

Carstensz Glacier

Carstensz Pyramide 16,500 ft.

East Carstensz Top

DUTCH 1936

Tsing River

Hammerhead 14,500 ft.

13

BASE 11,000 ft.

From Ilaga

The tussock route did not offer a clear path. It wound in and out and upwards under a canopy of bush: there was no question of climbing steadily. We were obliged to break away branches, trample down the undergrowth and squeeze awkwardly over and through the lines of tree trunks. The way would have to be improved with an axe and slasher for a laden party, but we were more concerned in reaching the top and pushing the reconnaissance than making the way easy. After an exhausting struggle, and well stung by nettles, we were faced by a dripping rock wall about twenty feet high. It was an outlying bulge of the cliff to our right. We pulled ourselves up and found an open gully of moss-layered rock which required step-kicking. Reaching an outcrop higher up I sat down and took in the view. The top half of the Noordwand was now visible, and the shining summits of Ngga Poloe and East Carstensz Top dipped in and out of the smooth banner clouds that clung to them as if nailed by the wind. Below Lynn the slope fell sheer away to the congealed surface of the lake.

At the top of the gully a further struggle through roots and branches brought us to the final slopes leading to the notch. The ground became broken near the top with karst and fissures. On the crest of the notch we stopped to regain our breath and to absorb yet another revelation.

A huge basin, a minor plateau, rolled to the foot of the Noordwand which leapt vertically 4,000 feet into the sky. Another large lake lay at our feet lapping the low hills atop the cliffs. The whole scene was one of bleakness, almost devoid of vegetation. A sharp, cold breeze sprang up as we stood and gazed at the great wall. It rose abruptly from beneath the summit of East Carstensz Top with no gentle slopes or curving ridges to temper the dominance of the precipice. It stretched unbroken to the west save for a high abutting ridge which hid its farthest extremities. Its crest was layered with ice, which we estimated to be at least 200 feet thick from our vantage point two miles away. The lip of the ice edged slightly over the top, broken and cracked, but did not cascade in icefalls and labyrinths of séracs. It was dead: the cold remnant of glaciers that once flowed through the basins we were exploring.

There were no signs of activity, no crumbled debris on the wall or smooth gullies showing the recent passage of ice.

As the sky greyed and scuds of mist began to curl over the summits and around the great buttresses the pressing question was: How can we get up the Noordwand and over the glaciers to the Pyramide? Our hope was that a glacier tongue descended between East Carstensz Top and Ngga Poloe, but as we were not in a position to see that point we moved down the slope into the basin and walked to the south once more along the edge of the lake. There was a cold magnificence about the inhospitable scene. The rearing rock stood aloof and held an antipathy to life and movement; it seemed a frozen, grand epitome of the elemental isolation of the island.

The lake in front was almost split in two by a knob of rock which reduced its width to a channel a few feet wide. We were tempted to step over and circle the basin to its farther reaches, but the great gap that lay between the edge of the Noordwand and the range we had climbed to its east demanded all our attention. Our eyes searched for a weakness in the wall's defences. With some excitement we noticed a tongue of ice to the south-west: it broke the line of buttresses and dipped to a point only a few hundred feet above the basin floor. This would almost certainly offer a route to the icecap, and with this sight we counted our reconnaissance almost complete.

The sun had gone and we walked towards a wall of grey cloud filling the gap. The lake pushed hard beneath the eastern range and we were forced to climb carefully along its very edge below the great overhang marking the limit of the range. We emerged on its southern side and saw that we were on a level with the crumbling buttresses that we had looked down yesterday. The upper part of the south wall disappeared into the cloud. The great gap was formed by the absence of any continuation of this upper section: it was as if it had been neatly sliced away from the landscape to preserve the unbroken sweep of the Noordwand. In hope of seeing beyond the gap we trudged up the steep rise to its edge, though the view had been reduced to nil. Our height must have been close to 12,500 feet. Before we had travelled much farther we felt a hint of rain in the air and chose a sheltered spot to have lunch before being enveloped in a downpour.

A vicious hailstorm burst over us. Soon our clothes were running with water as the cold, sharp hailstones bit into our faces and hands. We were frozen to the marrow and there was not much deliberation before we set off for home. We turned for a last look as a hole was blown in the cloud revealing the tongue of ice peering over a horrible, fissured wall. There was only one way to the top—by the break we had seen earlier. Released by the hailstorm, jets and cascades of water poured off the Noordwand. We shivered as we imagined the rushing winds, laden with hail, that were battering the glacier above, and the prospects of pleasurable climbing or even the establishment of secure camps were dimmed.

We moved quickly across the basin, enjoying the strenuous pulls over rock steps which forced our limbs to exertion and warmth. A waterfall gushed from a hole in a slab of grey limestone that had been perfectly dry when we passed only an hour before. Everywhere springs and trickles of water poured through the sieve-like rock. We mentally noted that camp sites would have to be chosen with care, since an unwise placing might result in our being assaulted by sudden waterfalls, or our tent cruising at midnight along fleeting streams. We paused as we approached the notch and decided that the lake was worthy of a name, if only for easy future reference, and since there certainly would be no native name we named it after the Ilaga pioneer—Lake Larson. A prominent peak on the western ridge beyond spelled its title of the Cenotaph, and the important system of three basins holding Lakes Larson and Discovery and the head of the river we called the Basins of Ijomba. Thus we hoped the memory of that great Dani would be perpetuated.

On the descent to Lake Discovery, Lynn found an easier route to the tangle of lower bush. The hail had stopped but as we entered the river basin, rain fell in earnest and even the most vigorous tramp towards the bivouac could not warm our bodies or relieve our saturation. We trudged along in miserable silence. The sight of the Noordwand buttresses briefly tearing the clouds apart did nothing to raise our spirits. The struggle up the bluff to the bivouac was exhausting and demoralizing. The rain mingled with waterfall spray and ran in unceasing rivulets down our faces, down our stiff, ineffective parkas, and over the cold, unyielding roots and rock.

The bivouac did little to warm our hearts with its pile of wet ashes and slippery sheet of plastic. I stood stiffly looking at the scene, holding my arms so that they would not press against the wet sleeves of my parka, and my head still so that it would not set off fresh trickles down my neck. I wriggled my toes to keep them warm in their cold bath. With a sudden burst of energy I threw off the pack and helped Lynn to peg out the fly before stripping and crawling into my down jacket and damp sleeping-bag. There was not a hope of lighting a fire, so we tucked into a cold supper and fell to mutual commiseration, deciding firmly at the end to eat a hot meal before we left for Base Camp next morning, come hell or high water. We already had the latter and our camp was hardly heaven!

That night I will remember as the worst of the whole journey. The ground beneath the fly became soggy as water seeped up through the turf. We were surrounded by an insidious infiltration of water as condensation formed on the plastic and began to drip steadily on to our covers. Coupled with this, condensation began to form inside the covers and gradually our bags became completely soaked. I shivered myself awake as the night progressed and cold coursed through me in long waves.

Daylight did not entice us into the open, where it was colder and wetter; we lay damp and lethargic until weak sunlight spurred us to movement at half past eight. Miraculously we found some partially dry tussock and persuaded it to ignite a mediocre fire. After much puffing and blowing we finally produced a warm though not fully cooked stew. This was followed by almost cooked scrambled egg-powder.

At 9.30 a.m., as we were poking the fire, there was a grumble in the distance that gradually grew into the muffled roar of an aircraft. The airdrop! We had completely forgotten about it. We sat stock still listening as the aircraft seemed to circle low in the direction of Base Camp. Whacko! We grinned, thinking of

K

tinned meat, fruit and, especially for Lynn, chocolate biscuits. I
had three cigarettes left. I had no need to conserve them now and
in an orgy of smoke I consumed them one after the other. After a
quarter of an hour of circling the noise of the aircraft died away.

We packed up two hours later, struggled into our clammy
shirts and set off for the valley head. One problem remained
unsolved. Although the approach to the Noordwand had been
established, a route for packing supplies to its foot had not. The
circuitous route we had followed on the reconnaissance was not
entirely satisfactory, since it would be definitely longer than a
direct, cross-country route from the Base Camp. It presented
serious obstacles to a man with a heavy pack in the two steep
bluffs and below the bivouac. Farther to the north an easier line
might be found across the gentler slopes near the Kemabu.

With this idea in mind we scrambled down the bluff, sidled
into the valley and walked northwards. The rain returned to
speed us on our way and we spared no look behind us we tramped
along the easy, flat floor of the valley. The tall tussock became a
little unmanageable as the valley narrowed and we climbed to an
eastern spur expecting to see flat plateau country beyond. Instead
we saw a disheartening complex of ridges and spurs liberally
clothed in bush. Farther north it seemed easier so we regained
the valley and continued on. We were pushed closer to the river
by its retaining spurs and suddenly it rushed into a deep gorge.
A *kanangda* lay at the entrance and from it a faint track ran up on
to the eastern spur. 'This is it,' I said. 'There's probably a track
all the way across to the lake.' But we were fooled: it led only to a
stand of chopped trees and then petered out into a mat of bushes.
Impatiently I stamped off towards the gorge and shortly we
crossed the river and climbed up the steep western bank. After
ten minutes of climbing laboriously up and down its precipitous
edge we 'threw it in'. A glimpse into the gorge's lower reaches
made us recross the river and head across country, come what
may.

We went across the grain of the country, and therefore
encountered all its vicissitudes. Our main obstacle was thick bush,
which crowned every spur. Between were streams ranging from

hidden torrents that rumbled under a canopy of scrub to open, distended floods that almost warranted the title of rivers. The bush was tough and unyielding. After following the easy gaps beneath the higher branches, zigzagging back and forth, we were invariably faced with the final task of bursting a way through to the next stream. Although exhausting, the technique was simple, consisting of the application of weight against the vegetation until either it or ourselves gave way. If ourselves, then a fresh line of attack was tried.

The bush grew thicker on the higher ground of the spurs and consequently we slowly lost height, inclining towards the main basin of the Kemabu, which became more and more apparent to the north. I was under the misapprehension that the Base Camp was by the Kemabu, and whenever I took the lead I turned more and more to its wide basin despite Lynn's urgings to keep high. This was almost our undoing.

We stopped for lunch when a sliver of blue sky appeared. We drank a welcome raspberry drink while a transient sun dried our backs. Feeling so tired, we craved the sunlight more than usual. I worked my shoulders in the warmth and found it pleasant to screw up my eyes against brightness instead of lashing rain.

An hour later the rolling spurs were still unfolding before us. As we topped each one and saw yet another beyond, unsettling doubts began to dominate our brief snatches of conversation. A huge outcrop of karst limestone stood over the Kemabu basin, fretted and carved like the isolated nave of some primitive cathedral. As the afternoon wore on we walked in silence, pushing on hard to find some sure indication of our position. We arrived at the rim of a gorge which presented almost sheer sides. I did not fancy the crossing and did not move until Lynn took the initiative and disappeared beneath my feet. Gingerly we clambered down, clinging to clumps of tussock and loose rock, until we jumped the last few feet on to a large boulder in the water. After straining against the strong current of the river we pulled ourselves slowly up the other bank and reached the top gasping for breath.

When we arrived in a shallow basin walled by a steep ridge,

we reluctantly admitted that we were lost. Nothing in sight was familiar, though I harboured a persistent feeling that the Cul-de-sac lay beyond the ridge. Although sure that we were lost we were equally convinced that we could not stay lost, since we did not have the means to spend another night out. We had no food, our clothing and our bags were saturated, and there was little likelihood of being able to light a fire. In my stomach I had a horrible empty feeling, which I had met before only when climbing, if I were stuck in the middle of a slope of unstable snow, or clinging to unsure handholds as the rock under my feet crumbled. Once more the sky gloomed.

There was only one move to make. Reasoning that we knew the outline of the ranges between the lake of Camp Thirteen and the Basins of Ijomba, we decided to walk due south until we struck some recognizable feature. At the top of the basin we might well see the lake or a familiar peak. I led off at a fast pace despite a tired tendon that kept nagging at the back of my right knee. As my watch showed 4.30 p.m. it became a tramp of desperation. A silly popular tune kept revolving round and round in my head. I stopped only occasionally when it was essential to regain breath, and felt that if I stopped long I should lose energy and heart.

Near the head of the basin some quirk of instinct told me to turn westward, and I did. We came to the basin's rim and looked down through the bush. There was the whaleback—and nestled on a shelf beside a river stood the dirty yellow of the tent. Beside it a pitiful fire sent up a thin column of smoke in defiance of the thin showers of rain which began to sweep across the valley. We looked in vain for the small Meade tents, the stacks of airdrop boxes and a scatter of food tins. There was nothing more than the tent. The airdrop had failed.

Feeling a terrible disappointment, alleviated only by our relief in finding camp, we descended.

IO

The Turning-point

When God made this place
He made mountains and fissures
Hostile, vicious, and turned
Away His face.

AFTER Lynn and I left Camp Thirteen on 24th June, the main
preoccupation of the rest of the party was to set up Base Camp on
the site chosen for the airdrop. Two bags of *mbi* were left in the
ramshackle *kanangda* for later collection if necessary and the rest
of the equipment and supplies were ferried down valley from the
lake.

The Base Camp site was particularly good. The tent was
erected on a dry, firm shelf lying above a wide, swampy valley.
When not swamp, the floor of the valley degenerated into pools
scattered on either side of the deep, slow-moving river. It was
thus an ideal surface on which to receive an airdrop, the next best
to soft snow, and it was felt that the impact of boxes falling from
200 feet would be well cushioned. The approaches for a low-
flying aircraft were equally good. To the north-west, from where
the aircraft would probably approach, the land fell away steadily
to the Kemabu basin and presented no obstacles for a long,
straight flight path. To the south-east there were similarly no
obstacles and the aircraft could fly out over the lake with ample
room to bank away before reaching the mountains. On either side
of the flight path the land was high, with the slopes of the whaleback to the south-west and the ridge embracing the Cul-de-sac
to the north-east. Although the plane would fly below the crests

of these ridges on its dropping run, the wide valley and the easy
exit gave plenty of latitude for error.

On Saturday afternoon, the 24th, and Sunday morning, three
large bonfires were erected, thatched on the outside to prevent
rain from damaging the dry interior and placed at strategic points
to give the best spread of smoke across the valley. Puttoh and
Duncan settled back in the Meade to await the drop, while Tim
and Dave set off late on Sunday morning to begin their reconnaissance of the Dajak Pass.

Judging from the little information gleaned from reports of the
1936 expedition, they thought that the best method of attaining
the pass would be up the Bakopa valley, a main tributary of the
Kemabu rising west of the Carstensz. Accordingly Tim and Dave
set off downstream following the Base Camp river to the Kemabu,
with the intention of reaching the Bakopa junction. They walked
along the western bank, blazing the fern-trees as they went. The
river, in the perverse way of the country, appeared and disappeared
at will, until it developed into a gorge with 'steep, unscalable
sides'. Two days later Lynn and I defied Tim's dictum by scaling
the unscalable, since this was the gorge we met late on Tuesday
afternoon! Later they reached the Kemabu and erected a large
cairn.

Continuing westward beside the Kemabu they soon found
their route to the Bakopa blocked by another gorge. This forced
them up country, across the lines of spurs. They found the going
much easier than we did on our higher line and revelled in 'open
savanna and fern-tree forest'. At lunch time the break in the
clouds that had permitted Lynn and me to climb the Hammerhead
revealed to them a distant but clear view of the Carstensz and the
upper section of the Noordwand. Able to orientate themselves
with this view they moved south-westwards towards the head of
the Bakopa, abandoning the plan of reaching the junction.
Towards evening, after crossing country littered with karst and
natural bridges, they approached a high, whaleback ridge and
discovered a *kanangda* near its foot. It was well they did, since the
only artificial shelters, the tent and the fly, were not available. It
is almost certain that this *kanangda* was the one in the valley

draining the Basins of Ijomba; at this point only the routes of the reconnaissance parties crossed.

Tim and Dave had the same trouble with firelighting. While Dave went off into the evening to establish a good route for the next day Tim bid him goodbye with the assurance that a piping hot stew would be ready on his return. Needless to say, no such thing happened. Many hours of struggle were required to provide a hot meal.

The next day they climbed along the whaleback until it merged into the soaring ridge leading to the Cenotaph. They overlooked Lake Discovery at the same time as we were sidling Lake Larson. Sheltered from the hailstorm by the Cenotaph ridge they received, nevertheless, an afternoon downpour as they trudged past a group of lakes towards the Noordwand. When the clouds permitted they found the Noordwand unbroken and sheer for two miles to east and west. They estimated that its height was only about 1,500 feet. The valley they stood in must, therefore, have risen to a considerably greater height than the level of Lake Larson, which we estimated to be approximately 4,000 feet below the ice.

They were tempted to climb to a saddle where the Cenotaph ridge fell and butted against the Noordwand, but with the problem of the Dajak Pass formost in mind they turned westward. This was a misfortune of the first order. Had they only ascended to the saddle they would have obtained a much closer view than Lynn and I of the tongue of ice that fell from the Noordwand to the bottom of the highest basin of Ijomba.

It was growing late. They had just enough time to look over the next ridge to the west before descending to a rock bivouac. The next valley presented steep cliffs on both sides with the final wall of the Noordwand to the south. The Dajak Pass lay farther still, and they decided that such a route to it would be feasible only to a climbing party lightly loaded.

Their supper in the rock bivouac was boiled 'marmalade moss water' with broken biscuits which prefaced an uncomfortable night amongst lumpy but dry tussock. On Tuesday they began to make their way back to Base Camp. They followed the valley down before recrossing the whaleback and were overjoyed to hear the aircraft arrive close by and begin circling. They assumed that the airdrop had been successful and spent the rest of the day after regaining the *kanangda* resting, cooking up the remainder of their food and gloating over the delicacies that were in store at Base.

On Wednesday they took a more direct route back to Base Camp and arrived just in time for lunch. But they were not greeted with a wholesome corned beef hash but a bowl of rice and the abhorred *mbi* and the moody acknowledgement of: 'Where the hell have you been?'

'C'mon, get up, you lazy b——!' Lynn's utterance of the New Zealand mountain greeting when approaching an occupied hut provoked no response from within the sagging tent. Pulling back the flap we heard a sad 'G'day' and saw Puttoh and Duncan about to consume a huge pot of rice, unflavoured save for a sprinkling of sugar. 'Come in. Velly good Chinese lice.' We groaned, but at least they had not prepared sweet potato for us.

We stripped off our clothes, which had reached a final point of saturation when we waded chest high across the river below the camp. There was at least this luxury in reaching Base: I could pull on the dry track suit and socks I had left behind, stretch out on a dry floor, take in the familiar, decisive tones of Duncan's voice and listen to Puttoh's latest inventive theories. The plan to build an airship to fly from Australia to the Carstensz had been eclipsed by a plan to dehydrate meat with the vacuum pump in his back garden. Somehow even the most abtruse talk centred on food. I could not help thinking how thin and gaunt in the face they looked. Our absence of a few days had helped to put them in a different light, and no doubt to them we did not appear perfect pictures of health.

As I gratefully pulled off my boots I said: 'Well, we were about a hundred per cent successful.' Within seconds the maps were pulled out and after careful consultation we were able to trace our reconnaissance for them. 'That's good,' Puttoh finally said. 'Tim and Dave went off on Sunday and should bring back information tomorrow that will give us a complete picture of the Noordwand. Not that it will be much use to us now.' The gloom of the airdrop failure settled as I forced down the last mouthfuls of dry, tasteless rice.

Duncan was particularly vehement about the indecisive effort that had been made to drop our supplies. Whereas it seemed to Lynn and me at the bivouac that the aircraft had been circling near Base Camp, it had in fact gone no nearer than five miles off and no lower than 3,000 feet above the plateau. Duncan was disgusted.

It had rained steadily at Base until about eight o'clock that morning, but by nine a good fire had been stoked up ready for lighting the bonfires. At 9.30 a.m. the sky had partially cleared, the rain had stopped and Puttoh and Duncan dived out of the tent on hearing an aircraft approach from the north-east. It could not be seen but they wasted no time igniting the bonfires with brands from the main fire and the judicious use of kerosene. They had 'three beauties belching smoke and within ten minutes the smoke was lying thickly right across the valley'. Impatiently they waited, and at 9.45 a.m. the plane flew closer, visible this time and heading, for a brief moment, directly towards the fires. But then it turned, circled vaguely to the north and wasted little time in heading for home. They stood dumbfounded as the bonfires continued to spill smoke into the silent air. The plane had not even tried to find them. As the bonfires burnt out, the ashes could well have been the charred remains of the two hundred pound notes that the 'attempt' cost us.

We were faced with only one course of action—to withdraw. It was unlikely that the twin-engined Dakota would return the next day for a second attempt. We earnestly hoped that it would not, since we did not fancy the prospect of losing another £200. We would have to return as soon as Tim and Dave came back from reconnaissance—our food supplies were beginning to run short. Our medical kit was sadly depleted, the lack of plaster and bandages was particularly noticeable. Such basic commodities as candles and toilet-paper simply did not exist any more. On top of that our clothing was beginning to show visible signs of disintegration. My socks were slowly rotting into holes and my trousers had begun to give up the ghost at the seams. The prolonged strain of living under atrocious conditions with inadequate food was also beginning to make inroads on us physically. We were all noticeably thinner and our stamina over the past week had begun to wane. The thought of making the march back to Ilaga, hungry, and without Danis to shoulder our loads, did not appeal, but we were hardly in a position to pick and choose.

Out of cigarettes, I turned mentally from food to tobacco. I tried to estimate the earliest time at which I might be able to indulge once more. Monday at the very earliest, and that was assuming that we reached Ilaga in four days and flew out to Wamena directly. They might even have cigars there! Once the subjects of our reconnaissance and the march back had been exhausted, the four of us began to dream dreams of a return to the Carstensz. If we went back there would be no airdrop. Instead a few score Danis would be used and we would persuade them to carry our supplies as far as Lake Discovery, and then, in easy stages, we could breech the Noordwand and knock off all the peaks! To think that we were within an ace of doing that, until the calamitous quarter of an hour that morning!

We erected the fly over the entrance to the tent to act as a vestibule in which we stacked all our sodden and surplus gear. I wrote up my diary, raising my head occasionally when the rain spattered in to annoy us, and looked at the fading, grey view. The camp-fire sent up a token vestige of smoke against the dull background of fern-trees and tussock. There was a full moon that night but we had to be content to imagine it above the cloud.

With increasing relief we began to look forward to going back. We were decisively thwarted in our aims and there could be no alternative plan. With that fact lodged in our minds we turned to the next best objective, which to us was attainment of the luxuries of civilization. Let's get away from the horrible, disappointing place.

The Base Camp and the surrounding grey ridges became the worst place on earth. Instead of being the climax of my plans and dreams, which had begun fifteen months before, the Base Camp of the N.Z. New Guinea Expedition, 1961, was the most dreadful anticlimax that I could have imagined. Even though the possibility of airdrop failure had been all too apparent after reaching Ilaga, I had never really believed that we should be let down. But we had been let down and it came as a numbing shock that left me listless and resigned.

I seem to remember that I spoke little during the remaining time at Base—my mind was preoccupied with seething thoughts that tried to find a way out, an alternative, a new field of action. But there was absolutely nothing that could be done except simply—go home. It was infuriating to think that our failure was due, not to physical barriers and obstacles, but to human error and disregard. Did the Dakota pilots, probably at that moment talking shop over a cool beer, realize the effort and worry, physical and financial, that the expedition had cost us? Something in my stomach seemed to twist every time I thought about our failure. I tried to turn the clock back to the day before when I had stood close to the Noordwand, but inexorably it moved on to the day after tomorrow when the painful homeward trek would begin.

The next day produced a steady downpour and the oppressive clouds matched our mood. While Puttoh and Duncan went up to the lake for a stretch of exercise and for the two kit-bags of *mbi*, Lynn and I indulged in our first complete rest day since Ilaga. We discovered that Lynn had carried a book with him all the way from Tiom. As the day progressed the book, *PQ 17*, was taken apart into four pieces, which circulated round the tent as we all read it in instalments. No one else had included reading material for the trek, although there was a good selection in the airdrop ranging from the *Iliad* and Byron's *Don Juan* to that expedition handbook *The Ascent of Rum Doodle*. We did have one other book, though it was hardly entertaining reading. This was *The Ship Captain's Medical Guide*, a tome that Dave had carried for expert advice on how to treat our varied complaints from appendicitis to syphilis. It offered no comfort for bruised and cut ankles, which apparently have no place aboard ship.

Given our report on the configuration of the Carstensz and its surrounding ranges, Duncan was enabled to supplement his geological findings. Although the amount of research he was able to do was limited by our being always on the move, Duncan had kept an accurate record of the country we had travelled

across, with its main topographical features. He had a good
collection of representative rock samples and had made the
important discovery that a large area north of the Carstensz and
the other divide ranges was composed of volcanic and associated
igneous rocks. There were signs that these rocks were a source of
metalliferous mineralization, amply supported by the discovery of
gold in the headwaters of the West Baliem. The current belief
that the mountains of the island ran in one continuous divide was
discounted by Duncan's realization that a series of ranges ran
from the Carstensz to the Grand Baliem in echelon, thus:

Carstensz Range

Baliem Ranges   ↑
                                                    S

Apart from that he found evidence of extensive glaciation north
of the main ranges. An icecap nearly 400 square miles in area
existed on the Kemabu plateau during the Great Ice Age. Duncan
could feel happier than the rest of us. Puttoh had been denied the
opportunity to survey, Dave's plant-collecting opportunities had
been few (and far between), all of us had been unable to climb,
but Duncan had obtained some valuable geological results. They
were good to see.

Tim and Dave arrived back at 2.30 p.m. We re-erected the fly
and then crowded into the tent to hear the news. The rest of the
day was spent in cooking up *mbi*. We even went to the trouble of
a little sprucing up. Duncan presented the epitome of the 'philosophical attitude' as he squatted comfortably by the tent flap,
carefully combing his beard.

On Thursday, 29th June, we rose at first light and wasted no
time in preparing to leave. While Puttoh cooked our farewell
breakfast, the rest of us sorted out gear for packing. Anything
that was not absolutely essential to the trek back was abandoned
—personal and party gear alike. Old socks, handkerchiefs, a

water-bottle and the party towel, now more begrimed than our faces, were thrown in the natural ditch beside the camp. It was decided that, to reduce weight, the floor of the tent would be removed and this thrown away with the fly, all tent pegs bar four, and the rope. The canvas bucket was abandoned and the remains of the medical kit removed from its heavy metal box and jammed into a light bag. We stuck to our ice-axes without question. They were not only useful as walking-sticks, but were the symbol of our mountaineers' ideals. For us as mountaineers to throw them away would have been as morally wrong as a sailor's scuttling his yacht on losing a race.

Although there was a modest pile of *mbi* left we agreed to leave this since its nutritive value did not warrant its weight. Our food supply for the trek consisted, therefore, of eighteen pounds of rice and twenty pounds of miscellaneous European foodstuffs (including the weight of containers). We had one and a half pounds of food each per day if we could reach Ilaga in four days —one less than the march-in—but the diet leaned heavily on white rice and there was no reserve. We divided the food and equipment equally between us and carried approximately fifty pounds each at the start.

Duncan and I cut sections from the fly to act as ponchos over our porous parkas. I tied my still soaking shirt to my pack to dry during the morning while I wore my track-suit jumper. We were ready at 8 a.m. and took our last look at the eloquent remnants of Base Camp—a little pile of left-behinds hidden beneath the tent floor. We stamped on the damp ashes of the fire and then stumped slowly down towards the river. The pack straps began to bite into our shoulders.

I I

Four Days

There's nothing yet in my canvas bag
As heavy as this swag.

THE mountains were settled comfortably in cloud when we reached the head of the Cul-de-sac. Rather than return to the lake and follow the Corridor we sought to simplify the way home by as many short cuts as possible. In fact we harboured hopes of leaving the plateau for good that day, though as the morning wore on our dragging boots showed the vanity of that idea.

After we had splashed our way out of the Cul-de-sac we realized that our chances of reaching Ilaga without complete exhaustion were minimized if we did not maintain a steady, easy pace with regular rests. To have tried to achieve a twelve-hour day of fast walking would have been futile and we would have been effectively cutting our own throats. Accordingly we agreed that every hour's travel would be rewarded with five minutes' rest and that at least half an hour should be devoted to lunch.

I changed into my shirt, which dried quicker on my back, and pulled on my parka as an attacking shower flew over the hilltops. We were soon across the next basin and the stream which rumbled in concert with our empty stomachs. Over the next hill we descended easily towards the first of the twin lakes, Yenengena Hokajogu, and our mouths began to water at the sight of ducks. The second lake had risen in level, and where before we were able to walk ankle deep along the edge we had to wade to the knees.

We stopped for lunch at midday before we turned off towards the overhang camp. We had one biscuit with a scrape of butter, a little mound of scroggin that was lost in the depths of my big red bowl and a smear of honey. We licked up every last crumb. This 'meal' initiated Duncan's catch-phrase for the rest of the trek: 'If that's lunch I've had it.'

The half-hour rest seemed far too short, and as soon as I dragged myself to my weary feet my thoughts were immediately centred on the possible site of camp. The *kanangda* beyond the edge of the plateau, near the Zenggilorong, was well out of our reach, and steadily our sights were set lower and lower as each hill appeared.

Although the ascent to the saddle to the east of the lake was hard work I seemed to have lost the ability to sweat. Apparently we had all achieved a perfect state of balance in the water content of our bodies: very little was taken in, save through our skins, and little was expelled. I paused to regain both breath and energy many times on the way up to the saddle, and but for a deep desire to reach Ilaga as quickly as possible I would have been quite content to camp at our old site beneath the overhang. On the other side we scraped our ankles on the karst and later sat down near the Kemabu tributary before tackling the steep ridge which separated us from the main basin. Here I finished my last reel of colour film.

We reached the crest of the ridge only by dulling our minds and concentrating fiercely on the next few steps ahead. At the top we collapsed heavily in the tussock for a brief rest and then pushed on through the confusing, scrubby country. The track we had to follow was merely a trail of trampled tussock and when this disappeared we spent minutes scouring the slopes ahead for some sign. Duncan had taken compass bearings on our journey in, and with the aid of back readings we were able to continue in the correct direction. We came across the remains of one of the Dani signal fires and from there we could see down to the Kemabu River.

A wind which had sprung up blew keenly up the basin bringing sheets of rain. The hill on the northern bank of the river looked entirely featureless under the lowering banks of cloud and nothing offered shelter for a tent. The river was higher and I cursed as I sat on the bank and gingerly lowered my legs into the freezing water. The bed was as insubstantial as ever, and as I breast-stroked across to the other side, paddling my feet against the mud, my boot sank into a hole and the current began to float me downstream. I made a frantic dive for a clump of overhanging tussock and by clutching this and digging the pick of my ice-axe into the bank I was able to heave myself up and out of the water.

I summoned up a burst of energy to try and return some warmth to my legs, but to no avail; then I was relieved to see Puttoh drop his pack and signal that we were setting up camp. For a while we searched for an old *kanangda* we had seen on the way across but soon settled on the dubious shelter of a gnarled tree for the tent. Without a floor the tent spread considerably wider; it gave sufficient room for six if two lay across the head of the tent and four lay lengthways with the toes of their sleeping-bag covers protruding from the door. We were crammed in nevertheless, but the advantage of imitating sardines was the increased warmth from six bodies in close contact.

Puttoh had taken it upon himself to be chief and sole cook for the return. This decision was not made out of his need to mother us but to see that there was a proper conservation of our meagre supply of kerosene. We had three pints left. Puttoh had with him the stove he used many times in New Zealand and Australia and he had narrowed down to a fine art the generation of maximum heat for minimum fuel. Though we had the native axe it would have been a waste of time trying to light a fire after our recent experiences. The pressure-cooker was a godsend in our tribulations; it cooked within half an hour a meal that would have taken twice as long by any other method.

We tucked into mounds of rice laced with traces of mixed vegetable and marmite and, the supreme delicacy, a slice of nutmeat. Duncan claimed the prerogative of scraping the pot. We sat back wondering vaguely whether we were satisfied or not. 'Pass the fruit cake,' someone remarked. 'Oh, I think chocolate biscuits would go down better after a rice meal, don't you?' asked Lynn. 'Agreed,' I said. 'But don't forget the coffee, Drambuie and a cigar.' Lynn disappeared out of the tent, but not in pursuit of our imaginary delicacies.

We wedged together comfortably and the prattle was soon gone as the tent's yellow light faded and the rain intensified. Tim seemed to rattle a gigantic newspaper each time he turned over in his thick plastic cover.

At dawn the next morning no one made the move to get up: a warm sleeping-bag was too hard to leave for the cold mist. Finally Puttoh dragged head and shoulders out and began to cook breakfast. I dozed until a bowl of rice sprinkled with uncooked rolled oats was thrust in my face, and this brought the awful realization that I would shortly have to pull on wet clothes and boots. Our preparations were filled with listlessness and a general reluctance to move, so that it was not until 9 a.m. that the last pack strap was tied and we were off.

As we neared the junction of tracks to Ilaga the muffled noise of an aircraft caught our attention. We could identify it as a Cessna by the engine note and we stopped as it began to circle in the clouds at the southern edge of the plateau. It would have been just our luck for Steiger to attempt a drop when we had left the area. But the Cessna did not stay for long. It flew off to the west and our hopes for unexpected manna from heaven died.

The forlorn skull on the track was passed. We trooped across the basin towards Solstice Pass. At the junction of the two tracks leading to Ilaga we decided in favour of the one we knew. The final slope to the pass seemed inordinately steep, so we took our second hourly rest at the top and sucked our ration of one acid drop each. We paid no lingering farewells to the plateau, the Noordwand did not reveal itself, the clouds glowered, and the rain pushed against our backs as we dropped down to the fern-tree hollow above the Zenggilorong valley.

At midday we made ourselves comfortable beneath a limestone outcrop which overlooked the big *kanangda* and ate the same meagre lunch as the day before. I had pulled a tendon in my knee, so while Duncan sorted his rock specimens I strapped up the knee with an elastic bandage. When we started again I was not sure whether the subsequent stiffness of leg was worth the

L

reduction in pain. Lynn's foot also required attention. His toe, which had suffered frostbite in the Andes, was beginning to protest from being continually waterlogged. Over lunch I peered, fascinated, through Duncan's magnifying glass at his specimens and the fossils they contained. The side pocket of his pack was full of them. On taking a closer interest I began to realize the extent and value of his pioneering work.

A downpour greeted our return to the track and we could imagine the rain greasing the log which awaited us across the river. We paused by a stream to mix a raspberry drink, our last, and we sat down only half an hour's travel from the lunch spot feeling no sense of urgency and lacking eagerness to go to grips with the river. There was no Ijomba to 'Nawok!' us on, no bobbing kit-bags fading down the track to set us an example and our loads were no incentive to movement. We could sense the Zenggilorong below, but it was not until we paddled down the final stretch of track towards its bank that its roar became fully effective.

The sight of the bellowing water spurred me to put into words the thought that must have been in everyone's mind. 'What d'you reckon we go across *astride* the log?' There was general agreement. We stowed our ice-axes in the straps of our packs and carefully stepped down the first few feet of roots before sliding on to the log. Sitting astride felt infinitely more secure than the first walk across, and although our trousers were soon saturated from the spongy moss draping the log's sides we edged safely towards the other bank with time to take a bird's-eye view of the river. The water rushed past only a few feet below our boots. I felt relieved at having the Zenggilorong behind us. The log formed a thin and tenuous link between the forest and the plateau; its absence would create a dangerous barrier to any future expeditions travelling from the north.

We had remembered the following section of track as particularly bad and our memories had not failed us. It had deteriorated further and we marvelled that it had not simply flowed away, having reached such a liquefied state. The sudden burst of animated conversation that had followed the successful river crossing petered out rapidly as we began the climb up the eastern bank. Our sterterous breathing would not allow expression of the multitude of curses and pithy comments that revolved in our minds as we slid and slithered up the slopes of unrelieved mud. We did not stop, though every muscle suggested a rest, but plodded steadily on, using branches and roots for handholds while our feet skated unreasonably from side to side. A fine rain-mist arrived to cool our tempers but Duncan found breath for a stream of abuse, which cheered us considerably and seemed to ease our own pent-up annoyance.

We straggled on to the open ground of the shelf and allowed ourselves a rest and the ritual of sucking an acid drop—in fact we had two each, since we felt we deserved it. The exhausting climb had sapped our reserves of energy and there was no protest when Puttoh suggested we camp on the eastern side of the shelf by a group of *kanangdas*, which offered extra shelter. Another twenty minutes' walk saw us there. The three *kanangdas* were not an impressive sight. Two had been burnt down and the third collapsed by a fallen tree. We made some half-hearted efforts at repairing them but gave up as most of the main spars were covered in charcoal. Instead we pitched the damp tent before the collapsed *kanangda*, in which Dave elected to sleep in order to ease the crush. Since we had stopped early we had time to collect brushwood to soften our beds, and to create a barrier against the all-pervading dampness. We even made an attempt to light a fire. It was a miserable failure and we fell back on Puttoh's skill with the primus.

We tucked into two bowls of rice each that night, the second mixed with jelly crystals, which provided a welcome flavour and sweetness. My stomach was satisfied but my appetite was not. I longed for a cigarette to dull its edge. Despite the steamy cocoon of a damp sleeping-bag, sleep came quickly.

Two days gone, two to go: only two more days to Ilaga if we could keep up our pace. But again, on Saturday, 1st July, we did not set off until 9 a.m. My eyes were filled with sleep and my legs leaden, but my slow movements in preparing to leave were matched by the others. When I pulled my socks over my trousers, steaming dry against my night-warm legs, the wool of one had reached the final stage of rottenness and I rent a huge hole up the heel. My trousers were torn at the side and the main zipp of the down jacket had jammed. Even my track suit was smeared with mud and my shirt was thick with old sweat and incessant rain. I cleaned my teeth in a muddy pool of water for the first time in some days. That brightened the world a bit, as did a foaming mug of liver salts which we recklessly finished off.

Our packs were beginning to suffer. Webbing and lacing were rotting and Tim had to make do without a band at the small of his back when the canvas fell in two. Bedraggled and begrimed we set off, boots pinching and rubbing at our sores and bruises. Then the track welcomed us back to its mire.

That day saw the muddy monotony of the moss forest. There was nothing to mark the day as distinctive: it was a dull nonentity of a day, save that it epitomized all the worst features of the country—rain, mud, roots, moss and rain flowing in a liquefied pattern of green shadows and twisted nets of trees. The first two hours were spent dragging our reluctant limbs up the final slopes to the pass at the head of the Ilaga valley, and then a steady slog along the waterlogged ridge-top before we dropped to the Ilaga side-streams and gullies. My feet would not respond to a normal walking rhythm and sprawls in the mud or falls off logs became a regular feature of my progress. I accepted these without demur and could not even raise the energy to curse.

Puttoh saw our need for more food, and after only two and a half hours of travel we stopped on the site of our second camp out of Ilaga. The big *kanangda* was in good condition, and from the remains of the fire we could see that it had been used by our carriers on their way out. A stock of dry, splintered wood was lodged in the roof and with that we were able to build the first respectable fire since the carriers had left us. The bright, crackling flames were comforting as we crouched beneath the low roof out of the rain and sipped the last of our soup, stiffened by the inevitable helping of rice.

We looked over our supplies and found that we had sufficient food and fuel to last just three more meals—though the third one would be plain rice. We had to reach Ilaga the following night. The sight of depleted food stocks did not rouse us to any vigorous action. The fact was accepted and we lounged in the *kanangda* for an hour and a half until the rain passed. We cut wood to replace what we had used, then descended into the tunnel of moss.

The leeches were waiting for us and unobtrusively attached themselves to our hands when we grabbed bushes for support. The horrible creatures clung between my fingers, and without a cigarette to burn them away I had to flick them off, leaving a spot and trail of blood. We hurried past their restricted domain and crossed the first of the sandstone clearings as a torrential downpour fell to stir up the mud. We were sick and tired of rain; it began to seem so fruitless and unnecessary. It seemed a personal insult and degradation since there were no thirsty fields to satisfy, nor burning deserts to relieve. There was enough water in the soil to last the forest a month of Sundays. Such was the trend of my thoughts as I threw murderous looks at the grey skies and received a spatter of water in my eyes for my trouble. I pulled off my elastic bandage, which was proving more of a hindrance than a help, and climbed more easily across a deeply etched gully to join the others ahead.

The rain repented and allowed its sickly brother the sun to play for a short while. It was only 3.30 p.m., but Puttoh decided that the flat clearing we stood on was as good as any for camp. The tent dried out at an amazing speed in the brief sunlight; we were allowed to collect brushwood with our parkas off. When the ground was padded beneath the tent Puttoh shooed us into our bags and we found ourselves in bed before five in the afternoon, like naughty children waiting for our Spartan tea to be served as punishment.

The pressure-cooker and Dave's ice-axe were the latest casualties. The cooker did not hiss any more. It only gurgled through the valve, which was now effectively clogged with grains of rice. Its bakelite knob had disappeared and it was showing visible signs of strain under the mountains of swelling rice which it was repeatedly called upon to contain. Dave had caught the ferrule of his ice-axe in a tangle of roots that morning and the sharp crack that had followed was attributed to a shattered root. Instead a deep-seated break was found in the axe-shaft and from then on he had to lean on it with circumspection. The expedition was steadily falling apart at the seams. It was just as well that the mission was now only one long day's march away.

'Well, if that's dinner—I've had it,' remarked Duncan, as he licked the cooker lid. 'We haven't had the fruit cake yet,' protested Lynn. 'How about some peaches and cream?' grinned Dave. 'A tin of bully beef would do me just nicely,' said Puttoh. 'Oh, for goodness' sake!' I shouted. 'Can't you blokes think of anything else but food?' I covered my ears and wriggled deeper into my sleeping-bag, and concentrated on the fourth part of *PQ 17*. Our preoccupation with food was morbid in its intensity. Visions of delicious apple-pies and chicken became increasingly demoralizing. My stomach rumbled an added protest as I flicked over the dirty pages of the book and tried to imagine the hell of a wartime Arctic convoy, where they only had bully beef, biscuits and cocoa to sustain them. Only!

On the fourth day, as the light uncoiled mistily out of the night, we awoke to remember that it was probably the last day of our trek: the last lap on a 290-mile course. We struck camp a little earlier than usual and started off down the valley at a fast pace, eager to put the final miles behind us. We made good time until we descended sharply into wider reaches of moss forest, where we geared down to a steady stumbling through the trees.

We greeted each recognizable feature with increasing enthusiasm, and Duncan ticked off the miles in his notebook. He kept us constantly informed as to how many hours' tramp we had left before us. We clambered down the little wall of roots, crossed a main tributary, picked our way carefully over the subsided section of track and, over two hours later, we reached the site of our first miserable camp out of Ilaga. We shouted warm *koanas* when we saw a party of Danis slowly climbing up the track towards us. They were a mixed party of men, boys and women who were obviously migrating to the southern regions, since they carried a pig and *jums* full of their possessions. One clutched a bow and arrows. We told them briefly that we had come from the *dugundugoo* and they nodded, wonderingly. They resumed their steady plod southwards and were soon swallowed up in the trees.

At the bottom of the camp clearing was a deep stream, and the twisted sticks bridging it collapsed under Lynn. He fell waist-deep into the slimy water. Lynn's usual imperturbability was disrupted for the first time on the journey, and his sudden airing of expletives sounded a halt for lunch.

Early in the afternoon we reached the fertility symbol marking the extremity of the villages. We visibly relaxed when we looked across the ever-widening valley and saw cleared terraces through the trees. The day was growing more sunny, literally and figuratively, and everyone produced their cameras, which had been forgotten in the past days of rain and gloom. We stepped past the symbol, photographed a lonely skull on a post farther down the track, and entered the very last belt of trees before the main valley floor. We almost took the wrong fork in the track but a few minutes later we balanced along a dipping log and waded knee-deep across the stream.

Walking through the log jumble was our last ordeal. Puttoh celebrated the occasion by falling with a resounding crash on his back. The newly planted fields among the stumps were deserted. We realized to our dismay that it was Sunday, and that it would be difficult to employ Danis to carry our packs down to the mission—another three hours away. When we neared the end of the jumble a little boy appeared to peep at the muddy, hairy crew stumping awkwardly towards him. He ran to warn his elders, who were grouped to meet us when we finally entered the compound of the first village.

We threw off our packs and began attempts to recruit a group of carriers. The village headman squatted before us, head down and a wry smile on his face as he resolutely refused to shoulder a load on Sunday. Some women brought a small pile of newly roasted *mbi* which we quickly devoured. One small boy was fully prepared to carry a pack for us, and with his round face wreathed in smiles the little heathen slid under my pack, stood up and tottered down the track with the lower part of the pack webbing *under* his behind. This put one or two of the older males to shame and other packs were soon hoisted away.

Being relieved of my pack did not improve my outlook as it should have done. It had become an integral part of me, and without its stabilizing weight my legs chose a rambling route down the rest of the track. I clumped along its comparatively hard surface, suddenly the worse for wear. We soon had a train of followers, and two teenagers vied with my nipper for the honour of carrying my pack.

We filed through several villages, greeted by old men and women, apart from the inevitable throng of children. The young men seemed to be away—probably at a pig feast farther down the valley. Then we were greeted by a familiar figure, his arm raised in greeting: One-Eye. We shook hands with him warmly. He asked us questions, nodding in the direction of the *dugundugoo*, and clearly wanted an explanation of our early return. Again we imitated aeroplanes with waving hands and engine noises followed by a plop for the airdrop. 'Brrrr . . . plop . . . *lek*. Plop . . . *lek!*' He thought this was a great joke and we moved on comforted by the fact that at least someone derived enjoyment from an airdrop failure.

Grudgingly the final miles slipped past. They seemed to be the worst of all—the anticlimax of the expedition. My feet ached abominably as the day grew hot and sticky. I lagged behind while Duncan and Puttoh persisted in attempts to persuade the Danis to bring *mbi* and vegetables to the mission later in the day, but we did not strike any keen sellers and despaired at the prospect of another lean rice meal.

The cavalcade poured on before me and I had neither the energy nor the inclination to keep pace with the rush to the finish. Instead I plodded slowly on, leaning more heavily than usual on my ice-axe, and frequently stopping to savour the view—but only the view before me. I did not bother to look back at the forest, the rain clouds and perhaps the plateau. We had done with them.

In the late afternoon I passed through knots of curious bystanders by the mission house, and on descending the last hill joined the familiar scene of turmoil around our unfinished residence. Puttoh had arrived at exactly the right time. When he reached the hut beside our house Francis Titehalieu was in the middle of making a radio report to Sentani. When I arrived Puttoh had already arranged with M.A.F. that we would fly to Wamena the following morning. The mission was anxious to fly us out. Larson and his family were returning from the conference next day; we could use planes which would be empty on the return flights to the Baliem. A cigarette was now less than a day away!

The house had been improved in our absence. There was glass in the windows and doors to deter craning necks and prying looks. We dragged in our packs, threw off our boots, and enjoyed the first luxury of our return to civilization—no more walking. Although the Danis were eager to see us they had made no effort to bring food. Reluctantly I pulled out our remaining two pounds of rice and placed them on the bench alongside little bags of sugar and salt. Francis Titehalieu thrust his head through the door. 'Would you like coffee?' 'I'll say.' He brought us a bowl of hot water and a tin of Nescafé. Wonderful!

I sipped my hot coffee carefully, taking time to enjoy its flavour while Puttoh put the stove together. We told Titehalieu of the trip and it was good to have someone else to commiserate with us. 'And how are you feeling, Mr Temple?' 'Just a bit hungry,' I said with a laugh. 'Follow me,' he said. I stepped out into the dusk and crossed to his hut lit with a flaring Tilly lamp. It was comfortably arranged with two little rooms, the first dominated by the radio and shelves with food. My eyes almost popped as he pushed tins and packets into my arms: corned beef, soup, flour, sugar, instant pudding, rolled oats. He said 'Go and eat', and pushed me out of the hut. When I staggered into the house, delirious shouts welcomed the food and Puttoh speeded up his efforts to light the stove.

We took turns at washing while Puttoh cooked. In the 'kitchen' we had two galvanized tubs filled with water and we used one for washing and the other for rinsing. It was glorious to peel off the layer of mud which encased our legs and to douse our heads in clean water again. As I scrubbed my legs I noticed for the first time that they were considerably swollen: the product of ankle-twisting roots and bogs and the explanation of my bumble-footedness over the previous two days. Now I could stumble about in comfort, in a dry track-suit and basket-ball boots. Lynn's foot was in very bad shape and we realized the pain he must have been in when Duncan removed the dirty bandage from his toe and administered minor surgery to a festering sore.

By the light of two candles and with a second (borrowed) stove, Puttoh produced some massive pancakes which had us all gasping for air. We sat down and ate, stuffing ourselves with pancakes, rice flavoured with thick pea soup and sweet pudding. But it was too much. With bulging stomachs we had energy only to throw ourselves heavily on to our sleeping-bags.

Sated with food, we slept heavily and awoke reluctantly, gummy eyed, to a misty dawn on 3rd July. The first plane to fly us out was due in at 7.15 a.m., and while we sorted our belongings Puttoh was busy cooking a huge pot of porridge. The plane was limited to a 500-pound payload on taking off from Ilaga at over 7,000 feet; thus it was necessary to divide ourselves up into three suitable loads. After much deliberation, and working on the assumption that we had all lost a considerable amount of weight, it was decided that Duncan and I, the two lightest members, would fly out first with five packs while Puttoh, Tim and Lynn would follow later. Dave elected to stay at Ilaga a further day so that he could catch up on plant-collecting. He was also entrusted with the job of acquiring Dani souvenirs.

We learned that Ijomba and his carriers were still in Ilaga. They had not been able to return to Tiom, since they lacked the protection of a large party. They had told us quite clearly before-hand of their preference to fly back, and we could ignore this possibility no longer. Rather than see them spend an indefinite period stranded at Ilaga, we made arrangements for them to be flown home over the following two days. Puttoh, who saw Ijomba and the Irishman off that same morning, recounted how their faces were covered with wreaths of delighted smiles as they climbed into the Cessna cockpit, but added that their *kepewaks* made an awkward business of tying on the safety belts!

I sorted my pack before leaving for the airstrip and cheerfully threw away my trousers and socks, which no amount of washing would have renovated—though they are now no doubt some Dani's most prized possession. We were not sorry to leave. We were anxious only to reach a plentiful supply of food, beer and shaded comfort, which only serves to show how compelling is the human desire of creature comforts. The prospect of a longer stay in the centre of a primitive island with all its strange facets was no longer enticing; we sought the commonplace 'luxuries' of civilization.

There was a rush to reach the airstrip on time. We were not fully roused until Francis Titehalieu burst in through the door in his pyjamas to inform us that the plane would be early. Then came the first tangible sign of our return to the fleshpots—the panic to meet a time-table. We shouldered our packs and climbed the track to the strip above the mission. There was only a handful of Danis around the house and we dutifully bade our *koanas* for the last time. The view of the valley opened out as we rose higher, and the sun broke through the mists. Smoke sifted through the dark belly of the valley and the serrated rock peaks to the north scissored the clouds.

Precisely on time, we detected the hum of a Cessna. A wind-sock was hurriedly hoisted and we sat down to wait as the plane's shape became clearer against the dull background of forest. It made the customary circle to check wind direction and to see that control of the strip was in safe hands, and then landed. It was vitally necessary for a pilot to be sure that he would not be greeted by a native uprising. In the past natives had been known to stretch ropes across strips. One M.A.F. plane showed a battle scar on the leading edge of its wing, struck by a thrown spear when the pilot had 'buzzed' a strip to clear it of hostile tribesmen.

But he had only a group of weary New Zealanders to worry him this time. The pilot proved to be Hank. We helped him unload and then stowed the five packs into the back of the cabin. I got into the single deck-chair type seat at the back and securely strapped myself in. Duncan climbed aboard and we said goodbye to Mr Titehalieu. Hank thrust his long legs down to the rudder pedals, pulled the starter and we were enveloped in the sudden scream and roar of the engine. The plane strained and swayed as he revved the engine higher. He gave a sign and the chock stones were pulled away from the wheels. The brake was released and we shot forward down the strip past a flickering line of trees—a bounce, a final jump, and we were airborne. Ilaga was behind us.

12

Finale

But I'd cut a bit of a dash,
Buy a billycock hat and maybe
Go on the bash.

THE flight back to Wamena was exciting, both in the anticipation of the pleasures at the end and in retraversing the Baliem country the easy way. Duncan in the front was able to get a bird's-eye view of the country's structure, and periodically he would jump up and down with excitement as he discovered a feature which lent further support to his findings. We flew down the Ilaga valley a short way before banking due eastward to fly over the beautiful lake of the Vonkmeer, and then parallel to the West Baliem valley, which lay under a thick blanket of white cloud. Duncan shoved me. 'Look!' I swivelled round and craned my neck to look south-westwards. The Carstensz were clear, thrust up in an untidy jumble of blocks beyond the rolling hills of the plateau. Even the Pyramide was visible, our only view of it, rising above the curve of the south wall. I ached to be back there climbing on the ice. My eyes lingered on the distant summits until the swing of the plane took them from view.

Less than half an hour from taking off we were over the Meleri valley and at 8 a.m. we bumped along the broad airfield at Wamena. A strong, cooling wind met us as we walked to the Government hostel to book five rooms. We passed a few Danis but my cheery *koanas* met with no response. They were East Danis and spoke an entirely different language from those at

Ilaga. The hostel consisted of one long, rectangular structure built entirely of corrugated aluminium. The aluminium had been flown to Wamena in numbered sections and then erected on a concrete floor. The building was divided into a series of 'apartments' consisting of a small sitting-room and a bedroom with wash-basin. In the centre were two long dining-rooms backed by small kitchens with kerosene stoves for cooking. All the rooms were lined with hardboard. Behind the hostel were showers and lavatories; at the front a veranda, and a poor attempt at a garden.

All the other buildings in Wamena were of similar construction. In front of the hostel was 'high street', a bulldozed, flattened dirt road, with several aluminium huts and houses on either side. Some were a curious mixture of native thatch roofs and corrugated walls. Beyond the hostel and huts lay the airfield, which was fenced round but had no hangars or huts save a little shack in one corner. There were a few four-wheel-drive vehicles in the area, and a bulldozer, which must have been flown in and assembled on the spot. The Dani villages were some distance from the Government post but many villagers loitered around, eager to see each new white arrival by plane.

We pulled everything out of the packs and laid it all out to air. With that done I immediately inquired where I could obtain some cigarettes and was told that the local store opened at 10 a.m. I looked at my watch—an hour to go! We relaxed on the veranda and waited for the others, whom we expected at 9 a.m. But no more Cessnas arrived, and to the west black cloud was building up at an alarming speed. It was imperative that the rest of the party arrived by early next morning. De Kroonduif were operating three DC-3 flights from Hollandia the following day and we had the opportunity to reach the coast without delay. Anxious to find our airdrop packages and their delicacies, I looked where I had stowed them at the beginning of June—but they were gone: they had been taken back to Sentani.

Sharp on 10 a.m. I presented myself at the aluminium, windowless shed, which I had discovered was the store, and waited impatiently as the proprietor unlocked the door. Minutes later I pushed beer, biscuits and butter on to the table beside Duncan.

While he opened the cans I lit up a cigarette and coughed violently
—but enjoyed every minute of it.

As we rapidly sank the beer and biscuits we were approached
by two Danis, one of whom was carrying a magnificent stone
adze, which was obviously for sale. I quickly procured an interpreter and learned that a steel axe was required for payment. This
price seemed a bit steep, but the beautifully finished adze was
worth it. Followed faithfully by the two Danis, I found the store-
keeper, who had closed his shop, but he told me that no steel axes
were available. He suggested two knives instead, and since the
souvenir merchants looked interested we crossed to the shop and
offered two small sheath-knives for payment. There was a quick
dissertation between the pair, and then they renewed their demand
for an axe. It was no use telling them that there were no axes—
they had a fixation and were intent on driving a hard bargain. I
gave up in despair and they calmly trotted off to wait for the next
tourist, still not appreciative of the fact that they would not get
axes until the next shipment.

There were other expeditions based on Wamena at that time,
one from Harvard University filming in the lower reaches of the
Grand Baliem. Sponsored by the Rockefeller Foundation, they
were busy making a complete record of Dani existence, including
the wars in which they had become involved. A three-man
expedition made an unsuccessful attempt to make the second
ascent of Mount Wilhelmina during the period of our stay and
we were privileged to meet a member of the Archbold Expedition,
who was making a return visit to the valley, which he had been
one of the first to see. Wamena was becoming a busy place. Since
the hostel had been built there had been much traffic caused by
enterprising tourists and expeditions of all kinds. A short while
before our visit a Dutch parliamentary mission had passed
through on a fact-finding tour.

Puttoh, Lynn and Tim arrived just in time for lunch. It was
raining when we met them. Steiger was in a hurry, and after we
gave him a hand with refuelling he disappeared towards Pyramid,
the conference centre, to ferry some more missionaries home.

That evening we ran a party to which we invited Mr Schneider, the district officer, and his assistant. It turned out to be only a minor celebration. We had eaten so much during the afternoon that it was physically impossible to consume much of the carton of Dutch beer we had bought for the occasion.

Mr Schneider had complete jurisdiction over the Grand Baliem area, which had a population of 50,000 Danis. He had only three assistants and a limited number of trained native policemen to help him in his work. Apart from maintaining law and order he was expected to oversee road building and land development— an almost impossible task. There is no room for the maintenance of law as civilized peoples know it, with comfortable prisons, juries and bail. Force has to be met with force and the numerous murderers and warmongers in the valley receive short shrift. We saw a line of murderers labouring in chains and we heard of punitive expeditions to outlying villages, where killers were shot summarily when they attempted to ambush patrol officers. It was a hard rule but the only one workable where a handful of administrators were expected to control such a large, restless population. Much more could be done to spread education and agricultural development, but here, as in most other areas of Dutch New Guinea, education was left to the missions, and agriculture all but ignored. The primitive Dani will be hard to educate and civilize but a vigorous start should be made.

The night was restless from indigestion, despite the unaccustomed luxury of sheets and blankets. I viewed 4th July with a jaundiced eye but a still voracious appetite. We expected Dave to arrive early from Ilaga, but he did not. We prepared to board the first Dakota at 8 a.m. in the hope that he would catch one of the later flights. The chief pilot of De Kroonduif was piloting our aircraft, and it transpired that he had been flying the Dakota which had attempted to airdrop our supplies. We received a round of apologies, but the excuses given for failure—low cloud and hilly country—seemed insufficient when the pilot admitted to seeing our signal fires. No real attempt had been made; the flight from Wamena to the Carstensz had been squeezed in between normal schedules. We had lost over £200, which was hard to swallow, but to claim a rebate would have been almost impossible.

Moreover, our anger at the half-hearted attempt was spent; we were in a resigned mood as we heard the platitudes of apology. We strapped ourselves into our seats to enjoy the flight back over the Lakes-plain.

An hour later the New Guinea highlands were behind us and we were back at humid sea level. We found our airdrop sacks neatly stacked in a shed at the Sentani airfield, and as soon as we had dumped our packs at Jaab de Vries's house Lynn and I returned to ferret out the food tins containing fruit and fruit juice. We learned to our dismay that reports had reached newspapers in Australia and New Zealand telling of the airdrop failure; we were supposed to be stranded and starving in the middle of savage country. We immediately sent away cables to allay any fears and I began my final articles for the New Zealand papers.

The last days in Hollandia were a mixture of pleasure, illness and the dispiriting business of winding up expedition affairs. Dave arrived from Wamena on Wednesday with armfuls of plant specimens, which he sent away to New Zealand post haste for study before they deteriorated. However, De Kroonduif's air service let us down again and the plants did not reach Auckland until after Dave's arrival a fortnight later—all dead or dying.

Puttoh discovered that he had lost twenty-four pounds in weight in three weeks. His unplanned mode of slimming is commended as more effective than those widely circulated in women's journals. We had all shrunk, I least of all, dropping only fourteen pounds to a modest $9\frac{1}{2}$ stone. Our finger-nails had turned a sickly yellow from lack of protein, but we soon set out to rectify the loss. It did not help to be told by a well-wisher that released prisoners of war had died in the past from overeating.

At the beginning of July the New Guinea Council was in full session. This 'parliament' had been instituted some months before to administer Dutch New Guinea's internal affairs, while foreign policy and defence were still in the hands of the Dutch Government. Free elections had been held throughout the administered areas of the colony and the mixed assembly was constituted of Malayans, Papuans and Dutchmen, representing every section of the community. This was the first step towards

M

the ultimate independence of the colony—though our travel and contact with the peoples in the interior illustrated just how far in the future this would be. To create an independent state will require an extended period of vigorous education and development. Natives in the interior have no conception of politics and organized government. Many in fact do not even know that the Dutch exist. An ambitious project was described to me by a member of the People's Democratic Party, which I was told had branches in Biak and Sorong. This is a local, non-Communist organization. It desires an ultimate confederation or republic of Melanesia, thus forming the whole of New Guinea and the surrounding islands into one independent nation. A very grand scheme, and surely more desirable than separate independence of each small island or colony, or their dominance by some new power. With United Nations guidance that plan might offer a settlement of the area's problems.

We paid our £200 airdrop bill with some reluctance, and on Sunday morning we bid Jaab goodbye. Our first move took us by air into Australian New Guinea, where we spent a few days on the north coast before flying out from Port Moresby on 14th July.

That last flight, when we took off and crossed the coast of the Coral Sea, made a clear finale to our two months' stay in New Guinea. It brought back the early days of the expedition, when I first fingered the vague maps and wrote down the strange names —Biak, Wamena, Ilaga—tried to visualize the wild jungle, hostile natives, and peaks rising glittering and sublime over all. I could remember the tentative climbing routes I had traced on the blurred photograph of the Pyramide, when my mind ran riot with the thoughts of exploration in store. All the financial worries came back, the rush to send the freight on its way, the problems and the mix-ups.

Even clearer and closer was the final disappointment following the thrill of discovery. I looked back through the plane window as the high, crumpled hills slipped out of sight and Ijomba's face filled the scene, the slyness of the Old Codger and the grin of the Irishman. If we had not climbed the peaks we had at least enjoyed their company, savoured a simple way of life and chalked a new, wavering line of exploration on the map. But the pangs of disappointment were still strong. As I turned away I was presented with a glass of wine before lunch. I raised it.

'Here's to the next time!'

Epilogue—1962

I HARDLY thought on 26th June, as I absorbed the full impact of our airdrop failure, that less than seven months later, on 19th January 1962, I would once more stand on our Base Camp site and unearth the abandoned medical box and rope.

I was there under very different circumstances. Alone, with twelve Ilaga Danis, I was on my way to establish a Base Camp near Lake Discovery for Heinrich Harrer's Carstensz Expedition. From that date there followed a sequence of successes, profiting on the mixed chapter of failure and discovery which had been our lot in 1961. With the foreknowledge gained by Crawford and myself, I was able, before leaving Ilaga, to pick an ideal airdrop site in the Ijomba Valley, and the M.A.F. pilots had photographs of the site to guide them. On 24th January, 1½ tons of food and equipment cascaded out of two light planes in perfect weather with negligible damage and loss.

The main party of Harrer, Russell Kippax from Sydney and the Dutch patrol officer, Albert Huizenga, arrived a week later with a carrier train of 120. A big, comfortable Base Camp was established below Lake Discovery. Soon a wide trail climbed up to Lake Larson, beneath the North Wall to the west, and Camp One was set up below the promising glacier tongue first seen the previous June. But an easier way was found over the Wall. Harrer and Kippax discovered a pass, made ice-free by the retreating glaciers, which led to a beautiful camp site near the tongue of the Meren Glacier.

In the Carstensz area we climbed thirty-one summits—all bar Ngga Poloe for the first time. We measured glacial retreat, found the messages and camp remains of the 1936 expedition and on one unforgettable morning looked out to the Arafura Sea, our feet on ice and the sea fifty miles away and 15,000 feet below. The pinnacle of our success came on 13th February, when we reached the summit of the Carstensz Pyramide and so fulfilled an ambition which I had first dreamt of nearly two years before in Malte Brun hut. It was a magnificent climb and our most difficult, up rock chimneys, cracks and along a superb ridge rent with three ravines. It was fitting that the greatest mountain in Oceania should not be easy.

After that Kippax and Huizenga went home. Harrer and I made a trip to Idenburg Top, 15,600 feet, which we climbed on 24th February. It was a trip reminiscent of 1961, since we were forced to carry loads up to sixty pounds for five days when our carriers deserted. On our way to Base Camp for the last time on 3rd March I discovered the wreckage of a wartime cargo plane beneath Ngga Poloe. In 1961 Crawford and I had been within a few hundred yards of the wreck.

We left Ilaga for good on 21st March and set off to find stone axe quarries in unexplored country near the Lakesplain, but Harrer broke ribs in a fall and the trip was postponed. While he recuperated in Hollandia I walked from our base at Mulia Mission to Tiom. This took five days over partly known country before reaching the Meleri and our old track. The people at the head of the Meleri were still unfriendly but I did not suffer another attack!

I paused by the remains of our Camp One fire in the Meleri gorge and on reaching Tiom had a poignant and moving reunion with Ijomba.

At the time of writing I have another two months to go in New Guinea, during which time I shall return with Harrer to the stone axe quarries and then go on alone into unexplored country with uncontacted peoples. New Guinea has me under its spell and the vast regions of unknown, exciting hills and mountains with their primitive peoples are a source of constant wonder.

Wamena,
   22nd April 1962

An Assessment

I OFFER here a brief summary of the expedition's findings on plans, equipment and actions, in the hope that it may assist any future party that intends exploring and climbing in the Carstensz area and, in some respects, New Guinea as a whole. Firstly, planning and transport problems are dealt with, followed by advice and suggestions with regard to equipment and then by summaries of geological and botanical research.

Large or Small?

A small party is recommended for mobility and ease of transport. That is to say, if climbing is the chief objective, with scientific research playing the minor role, an expedition of four members is sufficient. The Colijn expedition of 1936 consisted of only three members, but the scope of such a party is limited in that it cannot be split to explore and survey a large area, and injury among such a small number would present serious consequences. A six-man expedition is equally as suitable as four men, since increased logistical problems are not noticeable while more exploration and research is possible. Beyond a six-man expedition costs begin to soar, the maintenance of an efficient transport system becomes the major preoccupation and a larger party is entirely unnecessary for the mountaineering problems involved.

Objectives

There are only four attractive objectives for mountaineering expeditions. Juliana Top, 15,600 feet, in the Star Mountains south-east of the Grand Baliem valley, was climbed in 1959 and offers no technical problems. There are no other peaks in that area worth the attention of an expedition and the march-in is extended and very difficult. The 1959 Dutch expedition, which had sixteen members, accomplished much ornithological, botanical and ethnic research but cost tens of thousands of pounds due to the wide and necessary use of aircraft and helicopters for supply.

Wilhelmina Top, 15,800 feet, has been climbed only once, from the south. Attempts by members of the 1938–9 Archbold expedition and by the 1961 party, both from the north, failed. For a small expedition with a limited budget it offers a worthy challenge. Although access is relatively easy, within four days' march of Wamena, it presents some difficult rock routes. Its snowcap has virtually disappeared, unlike Juliana Top, and it is exclusively a rock climb.

The Carstensz Toppen, up to 16,500 feet, are the highest and most interesting mountains in the whole island. The Carstensz Pyramide, which was the objective of this expedition, is the highest and probably most difficult climb, offering long rock ridges and high faces with glacial approaches. Ngga Poloe, the high glacier peak, has been climbed once, but East Carstensz Top, which would give a longer and more interesting climb, has not.

Idenburg Top, 15,900 feet, lies a few miles to the west of the Carstensz Toppen and would provide a worthwhile secondary objective to an expedition to the higher peaks. Little is known of it save that it would be basically a rock climb.

An expedition with modest climbing ambitions could well look to the Prinz Willem Gebergte, rising up to about 14,000 feet and lying about midway between Wilhelmina Top and the Carstensz Toppen. Access would be made from the West Baliem along the line of our trek from Tiom. It should be pointed out that the rock in all areas is fundamentally limestone.

The Seasons

Dutch New Guinea is influenced by two winds. The southeast trade wind is dominant from May to November and the north-west monsoon from December to April. Our expedition took place during the former period and experienced continual rain and cloudy conditions when in close proximity to the main divide ranges. During our stay in the Grand Baliem, at Ilaga and during the first days' trek up the Meleri, we experienced dry and sunny weather, but near the mountains we seemed to move within the limits of the south-east trade wind.

The 1936 expedition was in the Carstensz area during November and December, theoretically during the overlap between the two seasons, but still received a liberal supply of rain though generally better conditions than the 1961 expedition.

October to December is probably the best time, although the period March to May could well be investigated. Heavy rainfall can always be counted upon under windless conditions, graduating to hail and a little snow at the higher levels. Day temperatures above 6,000 feet are warm, though the temperature drops sharply at nightfall and mild to severe frosts can be experienced at higher altitudes.

First Moves

With party, objective and season chosen, the first preoccupations of an expedition are permission to go and that bogy of all expeditions and life in general—finance.

Permission should be sought at an early stage from Dutch authorities in the country of the expedition's origin and through them from the Government in Hollandia. Visas are required, a bond has to be provided to guarantee the expedition's solvency and health permits are needed for travel in the interior. If radio and firearms are to be taken, licences have to be obtained in Hollandia, but the authorities should be given adequate forewarning of the intention to take them.

Finance is the first major problem to be met. It is certain to harass the expedition treasurer from the very first glimmering of the intention to go to New Guinea to a time several months after the completion of the expedition. It is impossible to say exactly how much an expedition will cost since so much depends on its size, objects, capacity for Spartan living and the extent of its use of air transport. A simplified breakdown of our expedition costs will serve as a guide, however, though it should be borne in mind that much personal equipment and clothing was used and major items, such as tents, borrowed from the New Zealand Alpine Club.

	£
Food	155
Freight (with associated costs)	150
Air transport (including return fares from Australia and New Zealand and airdrop attempt)	1,360
Medical supplies	20
General postage and official payments	55
All other items (including all equipment costs and living costs in Hollandia)	360
TOTAL	£2,100

The costs were met by grants totalling £960 and by personal contribution. To help food and equipment stocks, commercial firms can be persuaded to part with products free of charge for the right to use the expedition's name in their advertising and for a supply of photographs showing the products in use. Book, magazine and film rights can be sold, but such contracts are often difficult to obtain and carry many pitfalls.

Maps and Information

There is a considerable paucity of both information and reliable maps. The only series of maps of the central areas that can be relied upon is that compiled from the U.S. Photographic Survey made in 1945. Even so these have notable drawbacks. Firstly, there are many portions of the maps which are blank due to the presence of extensive cloud when aerial photographs were taken. Secondly, the maps are not contoured, with the result that the relative height and steepness in hills and mountain ranges are impossible to gauge before actual contact. Thirdly, the meagre nomenclature does not necessarily tally with local language and names. For example, though the Danis knew of Kemabu, Zenggilorong was foreign to them. We found these maps of no use until the Noordwand was sighted, a recognizable feature from which we could reckon our position.

Authoritative information on the highlands is hard to come by.

There have been few travellers. Only two books have been published that are of use to parties approaching the Carstensz area. The first is the account of the 1936 expedition by Dr A. H. Colijn, *Naar de Eeuwige Snieuw van Tropische Nederland.* This gives a general description of the Carstensz Toppen, the southern approaches, and includes many useful photographs. There is no information pertaining to the Kemabu plateau and the northern approaches. The second publication is *De Bergpapoeas van Nieuw Guinea en han Woongesied* by F. M. Le Roux. This is a work of three volumes with many photographs, some of which illustrate the ranges to the west of the Carstensz. Both books are in Dutch and there are, unfortunately, no English translations.

Copies of the photographs taken in the U.S. air survey may be obtained, or at least seen, in Hollandia, but these are extremely difficult to orientate without complete survey figures and details. They tend to be more misleading than helpful.

There is no authoritative source of information in Hollandia, and the best advice is to go and see, relying on native guides for route-finding and the missionary on the spot for general guidance. Needless to say, there is much scope for a survey expedition.

Choice of Route

Judging by our experiences in reaching the range from the north, we think that the southern route might be the best after all—despite the jungle. But we must remember that, being the pioneers of a new route, we had the worst of almost everything— in transport, air supply and weather.

If permission can be gained to land at the C.A.M.A. airstrip at Ilaga, then there is no question that the northern route is best. It puts an expedition well within a week of the mountains and, during half the travelling time, open country is traversed and its nature is more rewarding both from a mountaineer's and a scientist's point of view.

If permission *cannot* be gained to land at Ilaga then it is a toss-up between the two routes from the point of view of time spent, though the northern approaches from Tiom offer more unusual and partly unexplored country. The northern route also gives more direct contact with Hollandia, whence every expedition must start.

Permission to land at a mission strip, whether the property of C.A.M.A. or any other mission, should be directed to the mission and not through the Government, which has no jurisdiction over the missions. It is hoped, however, that a Government post and airstrip will be opened in the Ilaga area shortly, and that would finally solve the access problem.

Air Transport

The use of aircraft and a highland airstrip is the crux of every expedition approaching from the north. Assuming that permission has been granted for an expedition to land at an airstrip, the problem is to fly in to it.

The airstrips will take only light aircraft and the only organization flying light aircraft in Dutch New Guinea, at the time of writing, is M.A.F. Landing permission and the co-operation of M.A.F. must be verified well before the expedition reaches Hollandia. If both are forthcoming then an expedition is fortunate and its basic transport problems are overcome.

If landing permission is forthcoming but M.A.F. cannot supply transport then it is suggested that a light aircraft and its pilot be obtained from one of the many commercial air transport concerns operating in Australian New Guinea. Whether a M.A.F. or an Australian plane is used, permission to use either must be obtained from the Government Aviation Bureau in Hollandia.

It is best to fly the whole expedition, men and supplies, in one flight to Wamena by De Kroonduif Dakota and begin the light plane ferry from there. This simplifies the flying problems and gives the expedition an advanced base from which to work.

Because our airdrop failed, this does not mean that aerial supply is a doubtful proposition in support of New Guinea expeditions. It does mean, however, that an expedition with limited funds for aerial supply runs a high risk of failure if all is staked on one or two airdrop attempts—after which finance runs out.

At least three major expeditions testify to the success and

efficiency of aerial supply, when finance is not a limiting factor. In 1936 a Sikorsky twin-engined amphibian was used by Colijn to make a reconnaissance of the Carstensz and later to airdrop supplies during the jungle march and on the site of the expedition's base camp. There is no doubt that the Sikorsky was instrumental in the expedition's success.

In 1938–9 the Archbold expedition to the Grand Baliem area would have been impossible without the Catalina twin-engined amphibian. Flying from Hollandia, Archbold landed on the Habbema Lake and the Wamena River and kept a huge party in the field for over a year through aerial supply. In 1959 the achievements of the Star Mountains Expedition were possible only through the unlimited use of aircraft and helicopters.

The two last expeditions cost tens of thousands of pounds. Our expedition cost a little over £2,100, and therein lay the turning of success to failure. We could afford only two attempts with light planes or the one attempt with a heavy plane, and that did not succeed.

To overcome the high failure risk facing an expedition anticipating aerial supply, with limited funds, there are two courses open. The first course requires one member of the expedition to be familiar with the country, or a cheap reconnaissance flight to achieve familiarity. In this way the airdrop site can be known before the expedition leaves Wamena. Good flying conditions and visibility can then be awaited and only one airdropping flight put in on a preselected site. This course has its drawbacks since aircraft might not necessarily be available on the day chosen for airdrop and much time might be wasted.

The second course is to avoid airdropping altogether. This would entail flying all supplies into the highland airstrip and carrying everything from there. This means a large, possibly huge, carrier party with the consequent problems of *kanangda* accommodation *en route*, food supply and the awkwardness of handling scores of natives on difficult tracks. The difficulty might be met in recruiting more than thirty or forty carriers.

If an expedition still prefers to walk to the mountains before receiving an airdrop, the following points have to be clearly remembered. Firstly, a wide, open and unrestricted dropping site has to be chosen. Secondly, provision should be made for much paraphernalia to attract a pilot's attention: smoky fires, Very lights, smoke bombs and coloured ground-markers. Thirdly, a radio is virtually essential so that contact can be maintained with the airdrop pilot for his guidance. Fourthly, a heavy aircraft dropping should be avoided since parachutes are a must, and such aircraft suffer from a lack of manœuvrability at low heights in hilly country.

The cheapest way is to employ carriers, but the best way, assuming only limited funds are available, is to make the airdrop beforehand with the guidance of an expedition member.

Dani Carriers

Dani carriers were readily available, up to twenty in number, at both Tiom and Ilaga. These carriers were willing to carry up to thirty pounds of expedition supplies plus their own food supplies for one week, all for the payment of one steel axe-head or bush knife plus the cost of food (this would amount to a palmful of beads per man). A *jum* and pandanus raincoat had to be provided for each man, and an axe for the whole party. They did not require packs or clothing, or any other supplies save matches and salt. Future expeditions should not increase payment, unless directed by the mission, since lavish wages could ruin local economy. If carriers are expected to remain in the plateau and mountain area for long, blankets and flys should be provided and possibly payment increased, but here the mission's guidance should be sought before making such provisions.

It must be remembered that the Danis will not be servants. They will contract to carry so much for so long to such and such a point for an agreed payment and that is that: they do not undertake to wash feet, cook breakfast or erect tents. A bargain is a bargain, made at the outset, and it must not be broken at any stage. If they do condescend to fetch water or light fires, then it is an act of goodwill; nevertheless, these tasks are generally done by young men or boys. The basic principle to be remembered is the 'payback'. If a pig were given to an expedition, for example, an axe-head would be expected in return. If a Dani is given beads or some present, he will give something in return—either a service or a gift. This principle at one time applied to their wars and vendettas: if one man was killed then that man's son or closest relation was bound to kill the murderer and the murderer's closest relation was bound to kill the murderer's murderer and so on indefinitely.

A headman will have to be found for the carrier party, and normally he will be a respected preacher or chief. The headman is not a commander, in the sense that he orders when camp shall be struck, who shall carry which load, and walks boldly at the head of the party. He is more an arbitrator, a guide to his own men as well as the *tuans*. He should be paid rather more than the other carriers.

Every consideration should be given to the Danis, to see that they have adequate food and that they are content with their lot. Although not at all accustomed to European foodstuffs, it would be possible to persuade them to eat tinned meat or fish, which they like, but not starchy bulk-foods such as rice or dehydrated potato. The provision of meat would help to cut down the weight of sweet potato, of which each man normally requires five to six pounds a day.

The length of the day's march and the subsequent camp site is entirely dependent on the Danis and on the site of *kanangdas*. Normally they will strike camp at any time from a hour after first light onwards, and will stop as early as possible in the afternoon before the onset of heavy rain. This stop could be at any time up to 5 p.m. if a suitable *kanangda* is not reached. No attempt should be made to force them beyond the point at which they wish to stop since this could result in unrest, desertion and also exposure if they were made to walk in heavy, cold rain. The Danis know best where good shelter and plentiful firewood can be found.

Equipment for March-in

Two factors have to be borne in mind when equipping: durability and, above all, waterproofness. In clothing, this means light but strong overall garments that will dry out quickly, and a parka impervious to rain. The parka should have plenty of room to avoid undue sweating and should extend to the knees. The correct choice of boot is particularly important. Put double-layer, rubber-soled climbing boots in the airdrop, for they are of no use on the march-in. Lightweight boots with sewn-in tongue and either calf-length uppers or leggings, to keep out the mud, are essential. They should be nailed and tricounied to grip on slimy logs and roots. A complete change of clothing should be provided for camp, and a warm body garment is essential, such as a down jacket.

One large tent for all *tuans* with an impervious fly to cover it is sufficient. The tent should have a strong, waterproof floor. A smaller fly for cooking and storage would be an added advantage.

Sleeping-bags need not be of Himalayan quality either for the march-in or for climbing camps, but should be equivalent to those of good quality used in the European or New Zealand Alps. Sleeping-bag covers, though used extensively on this expedition, should not be necessary if fly coverage is adequate.

Reliance should not be placed on wood fires at any stage. Large kerosene primuses are the most efficient for cooking and no more than two are required for a party of six. The general altitude justifies the inclusion of at least one pressure-cooker for the march-in.

Although described as 'a trap, a snare and a delusion' by one of the expedition members, ice-axes should not be left to the mercies of an airdrop. They may become entangled in roots and vines but are valuable as walking-sticks once open country is reached.

Equipment for the Mountains

At least two camps would have to be established above Base Camp at Lake Discovery before an attempt on a peak could be made. Therefore sufficient two-man tents must be taken to establish these camps. They should still be highly waterproof but need not be built to withstand strong winds.

Clothing will need to be heavier and warmer. It is recommended that strong leather gloves be taken to protect the hands while climbing on the limestone, which is often weathered into serrations, sharp knife-edges and needles. Similarly a good supply of rope should be taken to meet consequent high wear and tear.

Spirit stoves will be needed for high camps, but it must be remembered that cooking gasoline or 'white petrol' is not available in Hollandia and must be imported specially, through local oil company agents.

Medical

Anti-malarial treatment is necessary before, during, and for at least two months after a stay in New Guinea. A medical certificate stating that the holder is free from malarial, tubercular or leprous infection has to be obtained in Hollandia before entry will be granted to the Central Highlands.

The risk of 'tropical' infections and infestations is not great in the Highlands; on the other hand an expedition cannot rely on any outside help in a medical emergency. A good range of dressings, antiseptics and drugs, including antibiotics, should therefore be carried, and members should study their correct use. It is necessary to attend promptly to all cuts, scratches and blisters to avoid risk of infections such as tropical ulcers; unboiled water should never be drunk in or below populated areas. It is unwise to eat pork that has not been thoroughly cooked in a pressure-cooker. We saw no evidence of the existence of scrub typhus or of the mites which carry it; chloromycetin, which is effective against this disease, will probably be carried as a general broad-spectrum antibiotic.

The Dani carriers usually enjoy robust health, but they appreciate attention to infected cuts and burns. An ample supply of alcohol, antiseptic, sticking plaster and bandages should be taken for this purpose. Aspirin and salt tablets for the carriers are sometimes of value.

Photography

Although conditions in the vicinity of the Carstensz are usually overcast, the light intensity is usually quite high, and slow, fine-grained films can be used effectively. The continually

N

high humidity quickly leads to fogging of the lenses, malfunction of shutters, etc., and damage to the film both in the camera and in storage. Cameras, film and accessories must, therefore, be kept in completely impervious bags, canisters or jars with an ample supply of silica gel—which must be regenerated regularly.

Firearms

Firearms are not likely to be needed for self-defence between Ilaga and the Carstensz ranges, although they are very desirable in some parts of the North, East and West Baliem Rivers. On the high plateau below the Carstensz there are abundant wild duck and giant quail, which could be used as a major source of food for an expedition with time for shooting. The best combination of firearms for hunting in this country, and for defence if necessary, would be a 12-gauge shotgun and a ·22 repeating rifle.

Geological Summary

The geological objectives of the expedition were as follows:

(1) To make geological maps of the approach to the mountains from Ilaga.

(2) To map in detail the geology of the Carstensz Mountains and environs in conjunction with the topographical mapping to be done by C. K. Putt.

Because of the failure of the airdrop, the second objective was not fulfilled. However, the enforced march from Tiom meant that the scope of the mapping was enlarged considerably and, as a result, some significant discoveries were made.

RESULTS

General

The ground traverse from Tiom to the Carstensz Mountains enabled about 2,000 square miles of country to be mapped. The rigorous conditions of the trek, with the attendant lack of side-traverses, made detailed mapping impossible. With the experience gained on the ground traverse, the flight back from Ilaga, which was made in perfect weather, was very productive. A good idea was gained of the geology of a further 1,000 square miles of country.

Stratigraphy

The disposition of the major rock types in the area is now known with reasonable certainty, and they have been divided by the writer into several broad units which are given below:

AGE	FORMATION	ROCK TYPE
Pleistocene	Glacial deposits	Moraine, dissected glacial outwash fans.
Upper Tertiary	Ilaga volcanics	Andesite porphyry, agglomerate crystal tuff, marl, calcareous siltstone.
? Upper Tertirary	Meleri beds	Marl, calcareous siltstone, limestone.
Lower Tertiary	Carstensz Group	Organic limestone.
(Probable Unconformity)		
? Mesozoic	Ambum beds	Quartzite, quartz sandstone, micaceous sandstone, carbonaceous sandstone.

The ambum beds (upper Ilaga valley) are composed predominantly of fine-grained to medium-grained quartz sandstone of remarkable purity. In a more accessible location they would no doubt form valuable glass-sand deposits.

A discovery of considerable regional application in the area was that of an angular unconformity between the probable Mesozoic ambum beds and the younger Tertiary beds.

The discovery of the Ilaga volcanics and the associated igneous intrusive rocks was one of the major discoveries of the expedition.

They are Upper Tertiary in age and are probably correlatives of the diorite and porphyry intrusives mapped by Dozy (1936), south of the Carstensz Mountains. Alluvial gold originating in the Ilaga volcanics was found in the head of the West Baliem River; prospects were poor, and the discovery is probably not of economic significance except that it shows the Ilaga volcanics to be a source of metalliferous mineralization. The area between the head of the West Baliem River and Ilaga warrants further exploration for economic mineral deposits.

Glaciation

Glaciation north of the main range has been shown to have been much more extensive than was previously suspected, and the deposits of two separate glacial advances were found.

The older glaciation gave rise to valley-fill deposits up to 800 feet thick. They are mainly calcareous alluvial deposits and contain patches of moraine; they are deeply dissected by the later glaciation.

Extensive recent moraines overlying the older glacial deposits prove that the plateau north of the Carstesz Mountains was covered by an icecap at least 400 square miles in area during the maximum of the later glaciation. Other features such as glacial valleys, glacial lakes, cirques, etc., abound and were formed by the later glaciation.

Structure

A new concept of the structure of the highlands of Netherlands New Guinea emerged from the present survey. Folding is only of minor and local importance, except in the Carstensz Mountains, and the Tertiary rocks are generally sub-horizontal or only gently folded. In place of folding the rocks have yielded to the deforming stresses by large-scale faulting which the writer regards as mainly transcurrent.

The mountains of the main range are arranged in a remarkable and consistent *en echelon* pattern, and the writer has proposed a hypothesis to account for the pattern.

The samples of limestone and igneous rocks collected during the survey have been sent to the Bureau of Mineral Resources in Canberra for respective palaeontological and petrological determination. A report with plans is being prepared, which it is hoped will be published in the *Journal of the Geological Society of Australia* as soon as possible.

Hollandia,   D. B. Dow,
    8th July 1961.   *Geologist.*

Botanical Survey

Much collection was made for New Zealand research, both in the coastal area of Hollandia, the Ilaga valley and the Carstensz area. Preliminary tests were carried out for Auckland University on samples of bark and leaves likely to contain compounds of medicinal value, colouring matter or other chemical significance. Pressed and living plants which have magical, medicinal or edible value to the Papuans were also collected for the Auckland War Memorial Museum. Pressed snowgrass, live ferns and soil samples were collected for Canterbury University.

It was discovered through botanical research that there are no fish in the Kemabu, Ilaga, or West Baliem rivers, although there appears to be an abundance of fish food. The native carriers caught some fine crayfish in the tributaries of the West Baliem.

For the Pukeiti Rhododendron Trust, New Plymouth, rhododendron seeds, seedlings and cuttings were carried out by pack as well as various plants for the Auckland Parks Department. Rhododendrons were quite common in the north Carstensz area but only one species was found. In the West Baliem and Ilaga valleys, from approximately 7,000 to 12,000 feet, many similarities with New Zealand flora were noted. Colour slides were taken but the taking of these and other work was limited by the failure of the airdrop and the necessity to spend most of the time on the move.

Conclusion

Although our expedition failed to climb the highest peaks, we count it a success that so much was achieved within a few brief weeks. Much experience was gained in the mounting of an expedition in a land predominantly hostile in its nature, though the hostile characteristics we originally expected, such as snakes and poisonous insects, were never encountered: the country's hostility lies in its terrain and climate.

Perhaps the outstanding lesson we learned was that an expedition with our original objects was not fully practicable without the reconnaissance that our endeavour became.

> Dreams don't pay:
> There's no gold the easy way.

Christchurch, New Zealand,
    Christmas 1961.

Glossary

Awo, soon
Dugundugoo, general mountain area
Imay, here
Jum, net carrying-bag
Kanangda, wayside shelter or hut
Kani, fire
Kepewak, gourd penis-sheath
Koana, hallo, goodbye, thank you
Lek, no
Mbi, sweet potato
Nawok, start walking; get moving
Ndanda, long way off
Nogo, sleep
Paybi, long time coming
Petari, hair-net
Tuan, white man
Yenengena, lake
Yi, water; river

OTHER WORDS

C.A.M.A., Christian and Missionary Alliance
Chimney, wide rock fissure resembling chimney
Col, high mountain saddle—not necessarily a pass
Crayfish, freshwater lobster
Ferrule, spike and metal band at tip of ice-axe shaft
M.A.F., Mission Aviation Fellowship
Manyana, tomorrow is soon enough; plenty of time
Mountain Mule, frame pack made and used extensively in New Zealand and
  for expedition use
Noordwand, North Wall (Dutch)
Parka, waterproof jacket with hood
Rappel, method of descending steep rock with doubled rope
Scroggin, mixture of nuts, raisins, figs, dried fruit, etc.
Séracs, ice towers and pinnacles

Index